ROCKHOUNDING
Virginia

Help Us Keep This Guide Up to Date

Every effort has been made by the author and editors to make this guide as accurate and useful as possible. However, many things can change after a guide is published—roads are detoured, phone numbers change, facilities come under new management, etc.

We would appreciate hearing from you concerning your experiences with this guide and how you feel it could be improved and kept up to date. While we may not be able to respond to all comments and suggestions, we'll take them to heart, and we'll also make certain to share them with the author. Please send your comments and suggestions to the following address:

FalconGuides
Reader Response/Editorial Department
246 Goose Lane
Guilford, CT 06437

Or you may e-mail us at: editorial@GlobePequot.com

Thanks for your input, and happy rockhounding!

ROCKHOUNDING
Virginia

A Guide to the State's Best Rockhounding Sites

ROBERT BEARD

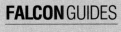
GUILFORD, CONNECTICUT

FALCONGUIDES®

An imprint of Globe Pequot
Falcon, FalconGuides, and Make Adventure Your Story are registered trade-marks of Rowman & Littlefield.

Distributed by NATIONAL BOOK NETWORK

Maps: Roberta Stockwell © Rowman & Littlefield
All photos by Robert D. Beard unless otherwise noted.

British Library Cataloguing-in-Publication Information Available

Library of Congress Cataloging-in-Publication Data

Names: Beard, Robert D.
Title: Rockhounding Virginia : a guide to the state's best rockhounding sites / Robert Beard.
Description: Guilford, Connecticut : FalconGuides, [2017] | "Distributed by National Book Network"–T.p. verso. | Includes bibliographical references and index.
Identifiers: LCCN 2017008737 (print) | LCCN 2017010314 (ebook) | ISBN 9781493028528 (pbk. : alk. paper) | ISBN 9781493028535 (e-book)
Subjects: LCSH: Rocks–Collection and preservation–Virginia–Guidebooks. | Minerals–Collection and preservation–Virginia–Guidebooks. | Fossils–Collection and preservation–Virginia–Guidebooks. | Virginia–Guidebooks.
Classification: LCC QE445.V8 B43 2017 (print) | LCC QE445.V8 (ebook) | DDC 552.09755075–dc23
LC record available at https://lccn.loc.gov/2017008737

CONTENTS

Blue Ridge

Valley and Ridge

Overview

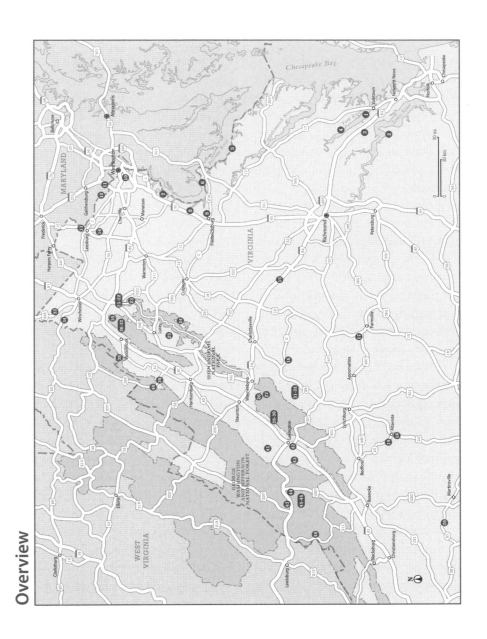

ACKNOWLEDGMENTS

Many people have helped make this book possible. I would first like to thank my editor at *Rock & Gem* magazine, Lynn Varon, who put me in contact with Globe Pequot Press, and William Kappele, another Rockhounding series writer and contributing editor at *Rock & Gem,* who suggested me to Lynn as a potential author for Globe Pequot in 2011. My writing experience with *Rock & Gem* has greatly expanded my capabilities as a geologist and has been a great asset to my career.

I would like to thank my editor at Globe Pequot, David Legere, for his encouragement and support for the book, and Melissa Baker in the map department, who gave me extremely helpful comments and suggestions. Thanks are also due to the production staff and the many people who were instrumental in producing and distributing the book.

In the course of this work, I had many useful discussions with state geologists and experienced collectors that I met in the field. I greatly appreciated the ideas and field discussions that I had with collectors, such as Ted Carver, and geologists, including Bill Kochanov. Jody Smale from the Pennsylvania Geological Survey library was extremely helpful with providing Virginia publications and getting me access to online resources.

While doing research for this book, I came across many books, websites, blogs, newsletters, and forums that gave excellent information on potential sites and often provided key information that enabled me to find difficult-to-locate sites. I appreciated the work of Jasper Burns, who wrote *Fossil Collecting in the Mid-Atlantic States,* and Keith Frye, who wrote *Roadside Geology of Virginia.* Websites from the Gem & Mineral Society of Lynchburg, the Gem & Mineral Society of the Virginia Peninsula, the Northern Virginia Mineral Club were a big help and provided great information for finding sites. I also appreciated all the support that my friends from the Central Pennsylvania Rock and Mineral Club gave when they learned that I was working on this book. I also owe thanks to the staff at Google Maps and the United States Geological Survey (USGS) who made the online mapping software and online geologic information that made this publication possible. Finding sites and determining the host rock geology would not be easy without these tools.

Lastly, I would like to thank my wife, Rosalina; my son, Daniel; and my daughter, Roberta. During the research for this book, they came with me on several trips as did my sister-in-law, Maria Tellez. I hope that you, your friends, and your families use this guide to find good field trips that become among your most memorable experiences.

INTRODUCTION

This book is for the rockhound or geologist who wants to visit sites without advance arrangements. Virtually every type of rockhounding trip can be found in this book. Some sites will allow you to park and pick up rocks as soon as you get out of your car. Other sites require some walking, and some sites require strenuous hiking over bad terrain. Some sites do not allow rock collecting at all, but are still worth visiting. At some sites you will likely find lots of minerals or fossils, and at others you may have to work hard to find anything. I have done my best to help you easily find these sites and let you know what to expect.

Virginia is a large state and is one of the most historic parts of the United States. More battles were fought in Virginia than in any other state during the Civil War. The region has some of the first mines and quarries that were developed in the nation. Many of these mines are all but forgotten and either developed, posted, or turned into parkland. While the region has a wide variety of mineral occurrences, as in much of the east, many of these are on private land or are public sites where mineral collecting is prohibited. Many famous fee collecting sites have also closed or were closed during the period of preparation for this book, and many are no longer accessible for mineral collecting. Some of the public sites that used to be open for collectors have become national monuments, and collecting is forbidden. However, the good news is that these government-owned sites are generally open to public access, which still is better than a private site that is not open to the public.

In this book I have focused on identifying sites that you can visit by yourself or with your family without significant advance planning or permission. I have personally checked every one of the sites in this book. I also went to many sites that were notable for their absence of minerals or fossils, and I have left those out of book. Many of the sites are roadcuts or outcrops that are somewhat limited in size but are reasonably accessible to visitors. Roadcuts are often within the highway right-of-way and sometimes belong to the state or local government. Generally you can collect in these areas if they are safe, not disrupting traffic, and clearly not marked against entry. For what it's worth, I have never had a problem with collecting at roadcuts, but I always make certain that I am not inside posted ground and that I am not in an area where I am posing a risk to traffic.

Interstate highways are illegal collecting sites, and I am aware of some mineral occurrences along interstates that are referenced in other texts that I kept out of this guide for that reason. It is discouraging to beat a site and have a police car pull up behind you, especially if you know you are not supposed to be there. Of course, land and access status can change at any time. Even if a private site is not posted, this guide does not imply or suggest that collecting at the site is permitted.

Many entries in this book are in county parks, state forests, state parks, federal lands, or other places that are accessible to the public, and while you can go to these sites, rock collecting is prohibited in many of them. Collecting shark teeth is allowed in many Virginia State Parks, but some parks prohibit any rock or fossil collecting. Collecting rules are not applied uniformly in many cases. If you look at the park regulations, you may find that any ground disturbance, including picking up a rock, is prohibited.

Many of these same parks and state agencies publish field guides to these parks. In these cases you will have to use your best judgment as to whether or not to collect rocks if you visit a site. If there are signs clearly stating "no mineral collecting," do not collect rocks. Likewise, if you are in a place where you know collecting is forbidden, you can look at the rocks, but do not collect them. Nearly all state parks, while offering excellent access to see former mines, quarries, and outcrops, do not allow any collecting, with the exception of some of the state parks that have beaches with shark teeth. Where an interesting mineral or fossil occurrence is on publicly accessible land but collecting is prohibited, I have still listed it in this book if I have visited it and consider the locality worth a visit. I have not yet found a site where it is against the law to look at the rocks.

I have stayed away from listing mine and quarry sites where you have to obtain advance permission and appointments, as many rockhounds often do not have the ability to schedule and make advance arrangements. Quarries and mines are generally best visited as a group with a local mineral club or other organizations. Such group trips to quarries could be well worth your time, as you'll bypass identifying landowners and permission issues. However, you must be sure to bring your own hard hat, steel-toed boots, hammer, and other tools that might be appropriate for the rock types you may encounter. Active quarries in Virginia are great collecting sites when you can get in, but many of the quarries are under new ownership and no longer allow mineral collecting.

For the rockhound with family members who don't love rocks quite as much as you do, this book also includes local attractions near each site. Many of these are local state parks, nearby lakes, and, in urban settings, nearby malls and cities. These should help you plan a trip that's fun for everyone.

Virginia is a big state, and it is nearly impossible to cover every locality. While I attempted to include as many sites as possible in this book, I found that the list of good sites kept growing, and eventually I had to draw the line on adding localities. The good news is that the more I kept looking, the more sites I kept finding. This is important, as it shows that there are still more sites to visit. I have never run out of new places to find rocks.

The best way to become a rockhound is to go out and look for rocks. You and your companions will see some interesting geology and places and have some shared experiences, which hopefully will be positive.

ROCKHOUNDING BASICS

Rockhounding can be a low-budget hobby. The entry requirements are minimal. All you need are your eyes and hands to see and pick up interesting rocks. However, as you advance you'll want some additional tools.

COLLECTING EQUIPMENT

A good **hammer** is the most important tool for the rockhound. I recommend a rock pick hammer with a pointed tip. Hardware stores don't usually carry these, but they are available at some surveying supply shops, at rock shows, and online. My preferred brand is an Estwing foot-long hammer with a pointed tip and a Shock Reduction Grip. I have used mine for over thirty years. It is almost impossible to destroy, despite thousands of whacks against very hard rocks and lots of time outside in the rain and snow. Do not use a regular claw hammer. The steel splinters that break off the hammer head when you hit a hard rock are dangerous. You should also be aware that similar splinters will often shoot off a new rock hammer when you are first using the hammer against hard rocks.

If you are hammering, it is also critical to wear **safety glasses or goggles.** I wear glasses normally to see, and my glasses have often been damaged by flying rock chips and steel hammer splinters. In the event that I am hammering large rocks on a constant basis, such as in a quarry, I will cover my glasses with safety goggles. When collecting in urban environments, rocks are often associated with broken glass, which becomes another hazard when hit with a hammer.

I also use a **chisel** to help break apart rocks when needed, but many chisels have very wide blades and are difficult to use when splitting the soft, finely bedded sediments that are common in many fossiliferous shales. I sometimes use a cheap **flat-bladed screwdriver** for soft shaly rocks where a chisel is too big to use. I know this is not the proper use of a screwdriver, but I have not found a better tool for splitting apart soft shaly rocks. Of course, if you try to use a flat-bladed screwdriver to split apart hard rocks, you really are then abusing the tool and run the risk of breaking the screwdriver or injuring yourself. When splitting harder rocks, the better tool is a chisel, and you need a narrow blade if the rocks are to be split along tight fractures.

Gloves are the next critical item. I used to do fieldwork without gloves but this is a dangerous practice. Make sure you protect your hands. All of us with day jobs that involve a computer are in big trouble if we lose the use of a finger or hand. Get a good pair of heavy leather work gloves from your local hardware or big-box store. Gloves are great when moving through briars, climbing on sharp rocks, and avoiding broken glass. It is easy to pinch your bare fingers when moving around large rocks, but gloves will help prevent this. It is better to get the end of your glove caught under a rock than the tip of your finger.

Get a good pair of steel-toed or equivalent **boots** to protect your feet. Having steel-toed boots is a requirement for collecting in quarries and mines, and it is easy to find and purchase a good pair. I prefer to have relatively light-weight boots. To find a pair that fits you comfortably be sure to walk in them before making a purchase.

A **hard hat,** while not needed for collecting at most roadcuts or places without overhead hazards, is equipment you should always have available. While you may not need one for casual rock collecting, you should have one with you or in your car in case you get invited to collect in a quarry or visit an active mine.

To say that you should have a **smartphone** is all but obvious today. Just a couple years ago I did not have a smartphone, but now I use one all the time. It has become critical as I use Google maps to find sites and give me real time data on my location. Frankly, I cannot believe that I used to go to the field without a smartphone. Today I cannot imagine trying to find a site without the use of satellite photographs and my phone GPS.

A **field book** and **camera** are useful for recording key site information. I like to record coordinates of sites and take notes of what I have found for future reference. I also use a small pocket-sized digital camera and often take hundreds of shots a day to increase my chances of getting that perfect shot. I use my smartphone as a backup camera, as I still prefer the pictures with my dedicated digital camera. However, I am sure that in a short time my digital camera will be replaced with my phone camera.

A **hand lens** to inspect mineral and fossils up close is also very useful, but if you are as nearsighted as I am, you can just take off your glasses and look closely. I recommend a quality hand lens that is at least 10× magnification if your natural vision is not sufficient.

Carrying your rocks from the site is often a chore. I like to use a small **backpack** when I have to walk a long distance, but sometimes a **five-gallon bucket** works best. A bucket is useful when you are picking up muddy rocks, and it is easy to put in your car. Just be careful not to break the bottom if you intend to also use it as a bucket. It is really irritating to fill your bucket with water and have it leak all over the place.

A **wagon** is good to have if you are working in quarries or places where you can expect to take out significant amounts of rocks. Collecting lots of rocks in a quarry is fine, as what you do not collect is just going to go to a crusher. If you take your wagon to a roadcut, you are collecting too many rocks. This can also attract attention from police and nosy people. Always try to keep a low profile and do not attract any unwanted attention.

GPS UNITS AND MAPS

Before digital mapping, I used to find every site by using topographic and highway maps. Now I use a handheld **Global Positioning System (GPS) unit** to record key site location information, and I use the coordinate feature on my car GPS to take me to the site. I still meet people who are not using all available features of their GPS unit, such as the latitude and longitude feature, so be sure you brush up on all the available features of your GPS. Now I also use my smartphone GPS and the satellite imagery, combined with real-time tracking, is critical for finding sites. I cannot imagine rockhounding without my smartphone.

Despite the advantages of GPS units and smartphones, you should always have **maps** as a backup. I like to have a state map, and I often get free maps at rest areas. I have also found my standard US road atlas works very well. Batteries can die, and satellite and mobile signals can be dropped in wilderness and urban areas where you do not have good clearance for satellite signals. Sometimes your charger will also short out. This happened to me on a multi-day collecting trip, and I felt like I was traveling blind when my GPS ran out of battery power. A good highway map can compliment your GPS and help make certain that you are not taking an incorrect road. Too many people have relied solely on their GPS unit and have taken roads that were not meant for for travel, especially in winter months. Unfortunately, many of these travelers died. If you get lost, most of the rockhounding trips in this book will not have such severe consequences, but never underestimate the value of a good map and never rely solely on your GPS.

If possible, you should also get **topographic maps** of your site. I used to buy hard copy maps, but they are expensive, especially when you are looking at several sites. I recently bought a set of topographic maps on CD from National Geographic, but unfortunately they have discontinued the CD series and replaced them with online maps. I found these to be completely unsuitable for my purposes, as I am often in areas without Internet access. I am hoping that technology and Internet access will improve to the point where I will access online topographic maps, but for now I am still working with my older copies on CD.

HEALTH AND SAFETY

Rockhounding presents many hazards that you will not encounter in other hobbies. In addition to having the proper gear, there are many health and safety considerations. Any time you go into the field, you are going into an uncontrolled and potentially hostile environment, and you need to take some basic steps to protect yourself and your collecting companions.

Sunscreen is one of the most effective and easy-to-use safety products, but many collectors still ignore its benefits. However, you need to put it on right away after you get to the site, or even better, before you leave the house. Many sites, especially the floors of open pit mines, act like giant solar reflectors, and the sun can be very intense. I also highly recommend a good pair of dark **sunglasses.** I cannot spend any time at all in an area of light-colored rocks if I do not have my sunglasses. Likewise, if you are not wearing a hard hat, wear a baseball cap or other hat for protection from the sun.

Although the sun is often an issue, rain is often a bigger issue. I highly recommend having an **umbrella** handy. I know it sounds ridiculous, but I have gone on many extended hikes in the woods in driving rain with an umbrella, and this helped a great deal. An umbrella can make a big difference in the quality of your trip, especially when you are with friends or kids that may not enjoy a soaking rainstorm.

Speaking of rain, **lightning** can be a significant concern. Many of the sites in this book are often exposed to strong thunderstorms and lightning. An umbrella will not help you if there is lightning. The best defense is to monitor the local forecast and get to a safe place long before the lightning arrives. Assuming you have a smartphone, you should be able to view radar maps that can warn you in advance of approaching storms. Your car will protect you from lightning, but bear in mind that most thunderstorms also come with strong winds, and you have to stay away from trees that can blow down on your vehicle. Every year people in the region are killed by both lightning strikes and falling trees.

Poison ivy can be a serious problem in Virginia. Poison ivy usually grows on the borders of outcrops and rocks, and this is another good reason to wear gloves. In fact, if your gloves have had extensive contact with the poison ivy, you may just have to throw them away.

While I always enjoy collecting in shorts and short-sleeve shirts, many sites are hidden among briars and other plants that can make your experience miserable if your legs and arms are exposed. I recommend always having a pair of **long pants** and a **light jacket** available if you need it, and you can also anticipate that these clothes will soon get ripped to shreds by thorns, broken branches, and sharp rocks. Long pants and sleeves can also help protect you from the sun and insects as well as flying rock chips and steel splinters from hammering.

Ticks are a major concern in the northeastern United States. During tick season, which seems to vary from place to place, I often find that I have been exposed to ticks as I am driving away from the site and see several crawling on my arms and legs just as I am entering traffic. Lyme disease is a serious issue, and you have to be on your guard at all times. The larger wood ticks, while not aesthetically pleasing, are typically not carriers of Lyme disease, while the much smaller deer ticks are known carriers. Rocky Mountain spotted fever, another serious tick-borne illness, is often carried by dog ticks, which are much larger than deer ticks. If you find a tick embedded in you, and it has been there for more than 24 hours, you may be at risk. Keep an eye on the bite mark, and contact your physician if it gets worse over the next few days.

To remove a tick, grasp the skin around the insertion of the tick with a pair of fine-point tweezers and pull straight outward, but be careful not to squeeze the tick body, as it may inject germs into the skin. Do not traumatize the tick with a lit match or cigarette. A traumatized tick can regurgitate its bacteria-laden stomach contents back into you. You will then be at greater risk of a tick-transmitted disease.

Using an insect repellant that contains DEET is a good defense, as is light-colored clothing so you can quickly spot and remove the ticks. But even with insect repellent, you can still get bitten. I received a Lyme tick bite in 2013 and had a bright red circle on my shoulder almost immediately, despite being covered with insect repellent. My doctor put me on antibiotics and apparently this took care of it, but I never even saw the tick.

Insect repellant with DEET is also good to keep away the **mosquitoes,** which may be present at any sites near standing water. Mosquitoes can also come out in force a few days after heavy rains. I have been on many trips that were nearly ruined because I did not have ready access to insect repellant. Insect repellant wipes are also good to keep in your backpack if you are prone to forgetting repellant or if you do not want to carry around an entire bottle of repellant. West Nile virus, which is carried by mosquitoes, is a serious threat. Spraying by state authorities has often dramatically reduced the numbers of mosquitoes, but if you are in an area that has not been sprayed and the mosquitoes are out, you will be in for a miserable trip if you are not protected. In extreme cases a mosquito net might be appropriate, but I have not been in any parts of Virginia where I felt a net was necessary, and insect repellant has always seemed to be sufficient.

An **orange or yellow safety vest** is important for any site where you are collecting along a roadside or any site that may be exposed to traffic or heavy equipment. Roads will always be dangerous, and many of the sites in this guide are at roadcuts. Provided you park in a safe place and stay well off the road, you should not have a problem, and the safety vest may alert cars to your presence. You should always make sure cars see you, especially if your back is turned and you cannot see them. An orange vest may be a state requirement if you are anywhere near a wooded area during hunting season. Generally I stay out of the woods during any gun hunting season. Curious onlookers may also assume that you are a highway worker or other employee just out doing their job and not question why you are so intently studying a roadcut.

Dehydration and **hunger** can make you and your companions miserable. Make sure that you and your collecting companions bring enough bottled water, and if you will be out all day, bring something to eat. Nearly all of the sites in this guidebook are near cities and places where you can get lunch, and most trips are half-day trips, so hunger is generally not a problem. Water, on the other hand, can be a problem. I generally have atleast one ½ liter of bottled water in my backpack and often take two ½ liters of bottled water, and make sure that my collecting companions also have bottled water. I know this sounds obvious, but it is not a good situation to be miles from the car and not have water for a thirsty person that you have introduced to rockhounding. Never, ever drink water from streams, no matter how remote or how good it looks, unless you are equipped with a proper filter.

Getting to the site safely is important. The parking areas for the sites in this book can all be easily reached with a two-wheel-drive vehicle. It seems obvious, but if you are driving to a site, be sure your vehicle will get you there and that you have **plenty of gas.** I always try to keep my tank topped off. Gas stations are relatively easy to find, but I do not like it when my tank gets low. If you are taking more than one vehicle, make certain that there will be enough parking for two cars. Many drives are also very long, so if you get tired, be sure to pull over at a secure rest area and take a break.

While many collecting sites are in somewhat rural areas, some of the sites in this book are in urban settings. You should always be aware of your surroundings, make sure your vehicle is parked in a secure place, keep your vehicle GPS hidden, do not leave valuables visible in your car, and be alert for suspicious characters. Generally, if you have a bad feeling about where you parked your car, you will find that feeling has been justified when you return.

Underground mines are generally a nonissue in Virginia, as most of the unstable mines collapsed or were closed many decades ago, and many of the open mines now have bat gates or other structures that keep people out. However, it is still possible to come across open portals and shafts, especially in some of the coal districts of southwestern Virginia. The best policy is to stay outside of any underground workings.

Finally, you have to be careful when dealing with sites on **private property.** Always ask permission when you can, and be prepared to get yelled at or have other unpleasant experiences with landowners. Many of my most unpleasant experiences have involved dealing with their large and quite vicious dogs. Nearly all the landowners I have talked with have been good about giving permission, but every now and then I come across unfriendly owners. This challenge comes with the hobby, so if you are going to look for rocks on private lands and ask their owners for access, you have to be ready to deal with difficult people.

IMPORTANT ONLINE TOOLS

Many mineral and fossil localities have recently disappeared into developments, yet in that same time frame it's become much easier to find new sites. Google, Yahoo, Google Earth, and Google Maps and other such online resources can be accessed to identify sites and explore potential localities.

I have found Google Maps to be especially helpful I always check the site using both the map and the satellite views. The map views are great, as they can show the street names and boundaries of public property, such as local and state parks. The satellite views are extremely useful, as you can zoom in and clearly see key items such as open pits, mine dumps, and signs of disturbance that may indicate historic or recent soil excavation and movement. Many sites, especially when minerals or fossils cover a broad area, are often exposed unexpectedly, and the satellite views in Google Maps can be a quick check to see recent exposures. Unfortunately these are not real-time photographs, and they are generally at least a year or two old. However, they are still much better than many maps and aerial photographs that may be decades old.

I have purposely left website addresses and phone numbers out of this guide, as web addresses expire, phone numbers change, and it is usually easy to find a web address via a search engine. Running an Internet search on a locality often brings up new and important updates, especially if a site has changed land status.

Likewise, all of the references cited in this book refer to the actual publication and do not provide a web address for access, unless the only available reference is the website itself. If you type in the citations or key parts of them, you can often access them online. If not, you can generally get them through your state library. I have found that a few publications are now only available on microfiche, but your librarian can often arrange for a copy to be e-mailed to you.

GEOLOGY

Some basic understanding of Virginia geology will help you understand why you encounter certain rocks, minerals, and fossils in various parts of the region. The area lies within five main geologic provinces, and this guide-book describes the geology of these provinces as opposed to just the geology of individual states. These are the Coastal Plain, Piedmont, Blue Ridge, Valley and Ridge, and Appalachian Plateau.

COASTAL PLAIN

The Coastal Plain covers eastern Virginia, and the deposition of the Coastal Plain sediments is similar to the deposition occurring on the coastline today. This province consists of a wedge of Cretaceous to Quaternary sediments that

The cliffs along the Virginia side of the Potomac River, such as this view from West-moreland State Park, offer some spectacular views.

overlap the rocks of the eastern Piedmont. The boundary between the Coastal Plain and the Piedmont is known as the Fall Zone or Fall Line. The Fall Line in Virginia traces a rough path from Washington, DC through Richmond, and south to Emporia.

The Fall Line is an important geologic feature that has had a huge impact on the history of the region. In the early days of what later became the United States, water was the principal route of transport. Once you left the ocean and headed to the interior, the best way to move goods and people was up and

Some of the Virginia beaches along the Potomac River, like this beach at Celadon State Park, are nearly deserted and can be dangerous in sudden thunderstorms.

down the rivers. Many of our big rivers became key trading routes. Rivers like the Mississippi, the Ohio, and the Hudson could be navigated along much of their route. However, boat traffic up the James River and the Potomac was stopped when they met the hard rocks of the Piedmont beneath the Coastal Plain sediments.

Many rapids and waterfalls occurred at the Fall Line, which, as its name implies, provides the sudden drop for the water to fall. These stops became natural places for settlements, and the associated waterfalls also had the benefit of providing energy for mills. Many locks were ultimately built to circumvent the falls, but of course this took a lot more time and energy, and in the meantime settlements could be established. West of this line you will encounter the rocks of the Piedmont and the other geologic provinces, and east of this line you will find the Coastal Plain sediments.

As you go eastward from the Fall Line, the Atlantic Coastal Plain sediments get thicker, and are more than 8,000 feet thick along the Atlantic coast of Virginia. These sediments continue to thicken as they extend to the edge of the continental shelf, which extends eastward for another 75 miles. The

Some of the Coastal Plain field trips in this book, such as the sandstone at Leesylvania State Park, can include a visit to the beach and a fishing pier.

sediments reach a maximum thickness of about 40,000 feet at the end of the continental shelf.

The sediments of the Coastal Plain dip eastward at a very low angle, and range from Cretaceous to Quaternary. As you head east, the sediments

Virginia geology played an important role in the Civil War. These cliffs at Alum Spring Park were reportedly used for shelter during the bombardment of Fredericksburg in 1862.

become progressively younger. Quaternary sand and gravel cover many of the older formations throughout much of the Coastal Plain. The older sediments are sometimes exposed in sections that have been cut either by streams, roads, or in some cases, canals.

Rockhounding in the Coastal Plain in Virginia is principally for fossils. The State Fossil of Virginia, *Chesapecten Jeffersonius*, can be found in the eastern Coastal Plain.

PIEDMONT

The Piedmont Province lies between the Coastal Plain and the Blue Ridge Mountains. The Piedmont is composed primarily of late Precambrian-early Cambrian crystalline igneous and metamorphic rocks. The province also

Windy Run near the Potomac River is a typical drainage in the Piedmont, and many of these are often steep and rocky.

includes Triassic sedimentary rocks deposited in basins formed by faults in the underlying crystalline rocks. The Piedmont extends from the western edge of the Coastal Plain to the long, northeast–southwest mountain range formed by Blue Ridge Mountains.

The Piedmont rocks, due their age and complex metamorphic history, can be difficult for geologists to map and understand. The lack of exposures

The metamorphic rocks of the Piedmont, such as these rocks exposed at Turkey Run, are much more resistant that the sediments of the Coastal Plain.

complicates the understanding of the Piedmont. Virginia Piedmont rocks lie within some of the most developed areas of the United States, and development has covered many of the rocks. Even outside the developed areas, the rocks are not well exposed, except in quarries and large mines for industrial minerals. Even the smallest outcrop can be important to identify the minerals and the structure of the underlying bedrock.

The Great Falls of the Potomac are a spectacular feature along the Fall Line between the metamorphis and igneous bedrock of the Piedmont and the sediments of the Coastal Plain.

The Piedmont is nearly flat with few topographic features, but the rocks are some of the most interesting in Virginia. Many key industrial mineral deposits, such as kyanite and feldspar, are within the Piedmont. Rockhounds can also find some interesting minerals in pegmatites that intruded the metamorphic and igneous rocks of the Piedmont. Many of the mineral collecting sites in this book are within the Piedmont.

The interior of the Virginia Piedmont, such as this area at the Scufflin Acres amethyst site, has abundant farm land and much of this is private.

BLUE RIDGE

The Blue Ridge Province is a thick group of Precambrian crystalline rocks and early Paleozoic sediments that lie between the Piedmont and Ridge and Valley provinces. This forms a relatively narrow section that extends from the

The Blue Ridge Mountains are among the most scenic in the United States, and you can reach many of these vistas from the Appalachian Trail near Compton Peak.

The Rose River is a typical stream that drains the Blue Ridge Mountains, and unakite and granite with blue quartz can be found in this area.

northern tip of Virginia into North Carolina. The Blue Ridge consists of a large overturned anticline with a core of Precambrian igneous and metamorphic rocks. The eastern and western flanks are slightly younger volcanic and clastic rocks. The Blue Ridge has some of the most scenic mountains in Virginia. Shenandoah National Park, one of the oldest national parks, is within the Blue Ridge Province. While collecting is not allowed within the National Park, the park has preserved many key geologic features. Many of these features extend outside of the park and offer some interesting opportunities for mineral collecting.

Rock and mineral collecting opportunities in the Blue Ridge Province include iron, manganese, blue quartz, and unakite. Iron and manganese mines often have limonite and manganese oxides. The blue quartz is found in gneisses and granitic rocks of the eastern Blue Ridge. Unakite, which is a decorative granite, with orange feldspar and light green epidote can be found in many of the creeks that drain the core of the Blue Ridge. Much of the area is either forested or developed, and it can be a difficult

This box turtle was seen along the Tye River on the eastern flank of the Blue Ridge Mountains.

This orange salamander was seen among the leaves and plants next to a trail on the western flank of the Blue Ridge Mountains near Pkin.

area to find rock exposures. Much of the area is mapped as within George Washington National Forest, but unfortunately many of the former mines and sections along the roads are private land.

VALLEY AND RIDGE

The Valley and Ridge Province consists of folded sediments that range in age from lower Ordovician to Mississippian. These rocks form a series of ridges and valleys that trend northeast–southwest. The ridges are formed by the more resistant sandstones and conglomerates, while the valleys are formed in the less resistant carbonates and shales.

Rockhounding in the Ridge and Valley is generally limited to fossils, but there are some small deposits of iron that can be good collecting sites if you are able to find and access them. Many of these iron mines were the iron source for the numerous iron furnaces that are found on the western side of Virginia. Most of these furnaces produced iron for the Confederacy during the Civil War. Many were subsequently attacked and destroyed by the Union

The eastern fence lizard can sometimes be seen on rocks, such as this one near the Fort Valley Road fossil site in the Valley and Ridge province.

Slag piles are found near most of the former iron furnaces, such as this large pile near Callie Furnace.

Folded sediments in the Valley and Ridge province are seen in prominent road outcrops, such as this outcrop of banded sediments near Rich Patch.

Army. Many were rebuilt after the War but technology and the vast iron deposits found in Minnesota and elsewhere forced them to eventually shut down. The fossils found in the Valley and Ridge are generally going to be found in the carbonates and shales, while the sandstones and conglomerates are generally not the types of rocks that will contain fossils. There are some sandy limestones and fine-grained clastic rocks that do have fossils, but these tend to be more the exception than the rule.

ALLEGHENY PLATEAU

The Allegheny Plateau Province is a broad uplift that has been dissected by streams and valleys. In Virginia, this province is located in the southwest corner of the state along the border of West Virginia and Kentucky. The bedrock of this region consists principally of shale, siltstone, and sandstone that are either horizontal or slightly folded. Several coal seams are found in the rock sequences as well, and many of these have been exploited by both underground and strip mines.

Rockhounding in this province is generally limited to fossils. Unless you are a local, this part of Virginia is relatively remote, and I was not able to visit any fossil sites in the Allegheny Plateau Province for this book.

NATURAL RESOURCES

Virginia was among the first states to be mined for metals and coal. The aggregates and building materials industry supplied stone for many important buildings in Richmond, Washington, DC, and other cities in the region. Virginia's diverse geology also provides a wide variety of industrial minerals. When collecting minerals and fossils, it is important to understand the underlying reasons for the location of mines and quarries. This will often help you identify the types of rocks you will encounter and give you some history lessons at the same time.

IRON

Like many of the original states, iron was the first metal to be mined in Virginia. Iron mining in Virginia dates back to the early 1700s. Bog iron was relatively easy to find in swampy areas of the Coastal Plain and iron furnaces were built to process this resource. The limiting factor for many mines was often the availability of charcoal for fuel and carbonate material for flux. The carbonate flux would reduce the melting temperature of the slag and remove many of the impurities from the iron. Along the coastal areas, some furnaces used oyster shells instead of limestone for flux, as suitable deposits of carbonate rock were often not available.

The bog iron ores were generally very poor quality, however, and while they contained iron, they were mainly composed of sediments and were ultimately too difficult to process into quality iron products. Larger, richer deposits of goethite and limonite were soon discovered in western Virginia. These areas also had abundant forests to produce charcoal and larger deposits of limestone to make flux. Many of these deposits provided iron for the Confederacy and the furnaces that processed the iron were destroyed by the Union during the War. After war, some of the furnaces went back into production. Iron production continued up to the early twentieth century at some of these mines and furnaces.

The goethite and limonite ores, while a slight improvement over the bog iron ores, soon found that they could not compete with the richer iron ores that were later discovered in some of the magnetite and hematite mines in Pennsylvania and New York. The discovery of these richer iron deposits quickly made the Virginia mines uneconomical. The vast iron mines that were then developed in the Lake Superior region ultimately doomed the Pennsylvania and New York mines as well. Today the remnants of iron mines in Virginia can be found in the forests of the Blue Ridge and Valley and Ridge provinces. Glassy slag is often easy to find near the old furnaces and along the streams near the furnaces.

GOLD

Placer gold was discovered in Virginia in 1804. The placers were quickly worked out and soon lode deposits were worked. Most of Virginia's gold mining was in the "gold-pyrite belt." This is a 9–16-mile-wide, nearly 140 mile-long northeast trending section in the Piedmont Province that extends from Fairfax County to southwestern Buckingham County. The largest concentrations of historical gold mines are in Buckingham, Fluvanna, Louisa, Goochland, and Spotsylvania counties. Other abandoned gold mines and prospects are scattered and are also found in the Blue Ridge and other parts of the Piedmont Province.

Gold mining continued up to the California Gold Rush of 1849, and began to slow considerably afterward. Many miners left for the California as the deposits in Virginia were small and difficult to work. Many of the mines in Virginia were undoubtedly worked by slave labor, as slaves were used to work the gold mines in the Carolinas and in Georgia. Production has already slowed by the time of the Civil War, and the Union Army destroyed what was left of many mines. After the Civil War, mining continued sporadically. In 1947, the last commercial operating gold mine in Virginia closed

Many people still find drainages to access and attempt to pan for gold in Virginia. Gold panning is a lot of hard work, and in my experience the returns have been minimal. You have to remember that many of these gravels, if they had gold, were repeatedly worked and worked until virtually all the placer gold was removed. In the meantime, the streambeds were further eroded and replaced with silt and lighter sediments that further covered any remaining gold. The old prospectors did not miss much, and it is very hard to find a place that has not been highly worked over. Still, gold has that allure, and at any given time there is probably someone still trying their luck panning for gold in Virginia.

COPPER AND LEAD

Copper and lead were first mined in Virginia in the mid–late 1700s. The last copper production was in 1947, and the last year for lead production was

1981. Lead and copper are no longer produced in Virginia. The copper deposits formed from metal-rich saline brines or submarine hot springs that flowed along fractures associated with rift systems or island arcs. The deposits were subsequently deformed by faulting and folding and further igneous activity and metamorphism. Copper was mined at many locations in the Piedmont and Blue Ridge provinces, and at a few locations in the Valley and Ridge Province.

In the Piedmont Province, copper has been found in massive sulfides in the Cambrian Chopawamsic Formation and as copper sulfides in quartz veins in the Cambrian Aaron Formation. It also occurs as copper sulfides and secondary copper minerals in Upper Triassic sedimentary rocks and as disseminated copper minerals in the Precambrian Alligator Back Formation. In the Blue Ridge Province, copper has been found in massive sulfide-, zinc-, and copper-bearing pyrrhotite deposits in the late Precambrian Ashe Formation, as copper minerals in fractures in the late Precambrian Catoctin Formation, and associated with granitoid plutons. In the Valley and Ridge Province, copper has been found in the Cambrian Shady Dolomite and in the Ordovician Beekmantown Formation.

Virginia lead was used to make bullets in the Revolutionary and Civil Wars. The most important lead deposits for bullets were located near Austinville in Wythe County and at Faber in Albemarle County. The lead occurred in zinc-lead ores within the Shady Dolomite and in the massive sulfide lenses in the Cambrian Chopawamsic Formation.

While important enough to be mined, these were still relatively small deposits, and no further mining for copper or lead should be anticipated. Nearly all the former copper and lead mines are on private land and cannot be accessed without permission.

COAL

Coal was first identified in Virginia in 1701 near the banks of the James River near Manakin (Brown et al., 1952). Virginia coal was mined in the Southwest Virginia Coalfield, the Valley Coalfields, and the Eastern Coal Fields. Not surprisingly, the first coal mining in Virginia was in the Eastern Coalfields. These are the youngest coalfields and occur in Triassic basins within the Piedmont Province. The Valley Coalfields are Early Mississippian in age, and the Southwest Coalfields are Pennsylvanian in age.

The Eastern Coalfields produced commercial coal from about 1748 to 1904. The Valley Coalfields had recorded production from about 1840 to the mid-1950s. The Southwest Coalfields produced coal from the late 1800s to the present day. The Southwest Coalfields are part of the Appalachian Coal Basin, which extends from Pennsylvania to Alabama and is one of the greatest resources of mineral wealth in the world.

The coal from the Southwest Virginia Coalfield is used for electricity generation, manufacturing coke, and supplying other industrial, commercial and institutional users. Coal is delivered by rail and truck to electricity generating plants and steel plants in the Eastern and Midwestern United States. Coal is railed to Hampton Roads, Virginia, the largest coal export terminal in the United States, and shipped to international users.

Unfortunately for the coal industry, the recent low prices of natural gas and oil also depress the price of coal. Electricity generation, which requires burning coal to produce steam to run generators, results in the production of particulates and greenhouse gases. Recent environmental regulations make coal much less attractive as an energy source. Energy efficiency has also reduced the demand for electricity. Coal will continue to be an important energy source for the foreseeable future, but coal mining companies and electrical utilities will continue to be challenged by low prices and environmental regulations.

Coal mines often produce voluminous mine dumps, and fossil plants can often be found in the dumps and on the hillsides of former and active mines. Minerals such as barite, sphalerite, siderite, and calcite can sometimes be found in coal mines as well. Unfortunately many of these sites are private, and the active mines are inaccessible without special permission. No coal mining sites or dumps are listed in this book.

INDUSTRIAL MINERALS

Virginia is known for the extent and variety of its industrial minerals. Industrial minerals are naturally occurring materials that are extracted for their commercial value. They generally are produced with minimal processing to reduce costs. They are exclusive of materials mined for energy, metals, and gem materials.

Materials mined for construction aggregates, dimension stone, and cement are considered industrial minerals. Aggregates and stone are among the most important natural resources in Virginia. The Atlantic Coastal Plain deposits have significant amounts of sand and gravel, while the Piedmont, Blue Ridge, and Valley and Ridge have several major quarries that produce stone for construction aggregates. Transportation is a limiting factor and most of the rocks produced by the quarries remain in their local market. The building stone industry, which is also known as the dimension stone industry, was very active in the nineteenth and first half of the twentieth centuries, and continues today. Cement is produced at a single location in the Valley and Ridge Province in western Virginia, and the lack of additional cement plants is largely due to the lack of other economic deposits of suitable limestone for cement.

Many individual minerals and mineral groups are mined or were previously mined in Virginia. Feldspar and kyanite mines are active in Virginia, and these are in the Piedmont Province. Other industrial minerals and materials mined or previously mined in Virginia include barite, clays, diatomaceous earth, gypsum, iron oxide pigments, lime, lithium, perlite, potash, sulfur, talc, titanium, and vermiculite.

Some of these mines, especially the feldspar and kyanite mines, offer excellent opportunities for collecting but they can only be accessed with permission. Virtually all active and inactive the aggregate, stone, and cement quarries in Virginia are on private land. Active quarries, while they are among the best places to collect minerals, are increasingly restricting access. Even the inactive quarries are often off-limits as they are on private land. The best way to see many former quarries is to find the sites on federal or state land where you can get access. These former quarries and mines on accessible government land often offer excellent opportunities to see rocks. While you can get access, you may not be allowed to collect rocks unless you get a permit or special permission.

HOW TO USE THIS GUIDE

The sites are listed by their location in the physiographic provinces, and are numbered westward from east to west and are grouped by geologic province. Site names are often based on the nearest town, but in some cases I have used a local geographic feature for the locality name, especially if this will help collectors with locating the site. Maps with the localities have also been provided to help you plan site visits.

Each site entry gives **GPS coordinates** for parking, and if necessary, coordinates for the site itself, should you need to hike there. The coordinates are the latitude and longitude and are provided in the degrees, minutes, and seconds format, in the World Geodetic System (WGS 84) datum. The coordinates are rounded to the nearest second. Enter the coordinates in your GPS device, and it will take your vehicle to the site. However, be aware that some GPS systems will take you on back roads and trails, and these may not be the best route to the site. In some cases, especially in rural areas, they may take you on roads and trails that may not even be made for motor vehicles.

Make sure that you understand how to use your GPS, especially when using coordinates. For some reason, some users know how to enter a street address but do not know how to enter a latitude and longitude. Sometimes latitude and longitude are given in decimal degrees or in degrees decimal minutes, and you have to understand what you are entering. You may have to do a conversion to the correct format, but this is very simple, provided you understand basic algebra. Often the GPS will give you a preview of where you are going after you enter the coordinates, and you should check this to see if it looks correct. If it is taking you out to sea, into a big field, or into a bunch of buildings in Wilmington, Baltimore, or Washington, DC, you may have entered the coordinates incorrectly. It is very easy to enter the coordinates incorrectly, but fortunately this is easy to fix, provided you catch it before you go too far.

The **finding the site** section can be a good partner to your GPS as you plan your trip. In this section, a route to each site is given from a major highway or, occasionally, from a nearby city. Depending on where you have started, the site may be between you and that starting point, so it is a good idea to supplement the GPS and these directions with a good state highway map.

I have personally visited every site in this book. The GPS coordinates were checked against topographic maps and satellite photos, and they are correct. In addition, the road directions in the "finding the site" entries were verified. The directions were originally obtained by the way that I went to the site, and then verified using detailed mileages and directions from Google Maps.

I often found that the location information provided in other field guides or geologic publications was either incorrect, too vague, or purposely left out to keep collectors away. I have also included GPS coordinates for both the parking area and the site itself for the locations that merit both. In many cases the parking area is the same as the site. In some cases you have to park and then hike a significant distance to the site. I sometimes had to visit a site multiple times before I found the right location, and even then I was sometimes unsure if I had made it to the right spot. You may use this guide and in some cases find that the spot I recommended was not as good as an adjacent location, despite my efforts to find the best spot.

The site descriptions can be used to quickly provide information about a site so you will know what to expect during your visit. The **site type** refers to the type of occurrence, and this generally is a physical description of the site, which may be a streambed, roadcut, former quarry, or outcrop. The **land status** is based on the best available information and should let you know if you will be able to access the site without special permission or if you need to secure approval from a site owner for access. In many cases the official status of a parcel is not known, and these sites generally have access but no guarantee that they are actually open to visitors.

The **material** refers to the type of minerals, rocks, or fossils that a visitor would likely find of most interest. If they are listed, I can assure you that they are present at the site, but it still may take some effort to find them. In some cases if a mineral or fossil is reported to be present at a site but I did not find it, I have listed it as "reported" if the geologic conditions are appropriate for that mineral or fossil to be present. Just because I did not find it does not mean it is not there.

The **host rock** is the rock in which the material is found, and I have generally named the geologic formation or type of rock that best describes the enclosing rocks as the host rock. It is important to understand what rocks host your materials of interest, as you can use this knowledge to find similar sites.

The **difficulty** level is a guide to the likelihood of finding or observing the materials referenced in the site description. Some sites are loaded with material and you can step onto the site and find as much as you could possibly desire. Other sites take hours and hours of effort to find a single specimen, and even your most diligent efforts are not a guarantee that you will find or observe anything. If a site is marked as difficult, be aware that it may not be a good site for impatient collectors.

The **family-friendly** rating is very subjective and depends entirely upon your family. If the description says yes without any qualifiers, you will generally find this to be a site where you can take small children and family members that can handle moderate walking and want to look at rocks. These sites also tend to be among the easier sites to find rocks. If the description says no, generally this is because the minerals or fossils are very hard to find, or because site access is very limited or difficult.

The **tools needed** field will let you know what kind of collecting tools you should bring to a site. In most cases a rock hammer and gloves are all that is needed, but for some sites you may be best served with a chisel, flat-bladed screwdriver, large sledgehammer, or shovel. At some sites, such in beach gravels that are screened, you do not need a hammer. I do not list standard safety equipment like boots, safety glasses, or hard hats here, as the emphasis is on tools. Unfortunately some sites do not allow collecting, so in these cases this field is simply "none." I usually bring my rock hammer, gloves, and day pack to virtually all sites, or at least keep all of them in reserve in the car if needed.

I have also included a section on **special concerns** so you know why this may not be a good site for everyone, especially if you are bringing small children, impatient collectors, friends, or family that may not appreciate the more adventurous aspects of rockhounding. This does not mean you should not take your family, but be prepared to deal with the issues mentioned in the site description.

If collecting at a site is not allowed, it is mentioned in the special concerns section. As mentioned previously, do not assume that this guide gives you permission to collect or access the property. In general, all public sites in this guide can be accessed and you can look at the rocks, but many parks and government sites do not allow collecting or disturbing rocks. If the site is private, do not enter posted areas without obtaining permission, and be aware that some private grounds are not often clearly posted against trespassing. In many areas ownership and the rules regarding rock collecting are not clear, so if collecting regulations are unclear at any of these sites, leave your hammer in the car and simply enjoy looking at the rocks.

Map Legend

Interstate Highway		Rockhounding Site	
US Highway		Capital	
State Highway		Town	
Forest/County Road		Mountain/Peak	
Local Road		Point of Interest	
Unpaved Road		Visitor Center	
Trail		Campground	
Railroad		Body of Water	
State Line		River/Creek	
National Park		Intermittent Creek	
State/County Park			

COASTAL PLAIN

1. Indian Field Creek Fossils

The beach on the north side of Indian Field Creek is littered with fossils.

County: York County
Site type: River Shoreline
Land status: Uncertain, may be state or federal land, but open to public
Material: Fossils
Host rock: Middle Pleistocene Shirley Formation sand, gravel, and clay
Difficulty: Easy
Family-friendly: Yes
Tools needed: None
Special concerns: Can be very hot in summer, clay is muddy during low tide
Special attractions: Colonial National Historic Park
GPS parking: N37°16′06″ / W76°33′22″
GPS Fossil Shoreline: N37°16′08″ / W76°33′27″
Topographic quadrangle: Clay Bank, VA

Finding the site: From US-17, take the Colonial Parkway 3.8 miles northwest, along the south side of the York River. The parking area is just before Indian Field Creek. The best fossils are on the north bank of the creek.

Rockhounding

This is Site 46 in Burns (1991). Collecting here is best during low tide. The fossils are mainly on the northern bank of Indian Field Creek, just west of the Colonial Parkway Bridge. This area often has many fishermen, and public parking is available just south of the Colonial Parkway Bridge.

The fossils here include pelecypods, gastropods, and corals. Shark teeth are also reported here but çwe did not find any. Many of them are exposed in abundance at the surface, and unfortunately nearly all of them are broken. It is difficult to find whole fossils. This is the type of site where you can spend a lot of time looking for the perfect fossil sections of the beach are covered in

Indian Field Creek is clearly marked on the Colonial Parkway. Parking is just south of the bridge.

The shoreline is thick with fossil pectens, barnacles, and oysters.

fossils and you have to be careful not to break the good ones. My patience and diligence paid off, as I found a gastropod and a coral.

The site also has hundreds of large granite and gneiss boulders along the bank of the York River on both sides of Indian Field Creek. These are used for erosion control and many fishermen use them as a stable place for bank fishing. Many of the boulders have large phenocrysts of feldspar, coarse-grained amphiboles, pyritic zones, and other interesting igneous and metamorphic minerals.

References: Burns, 1991; USGS, 2005

Sites 1–4

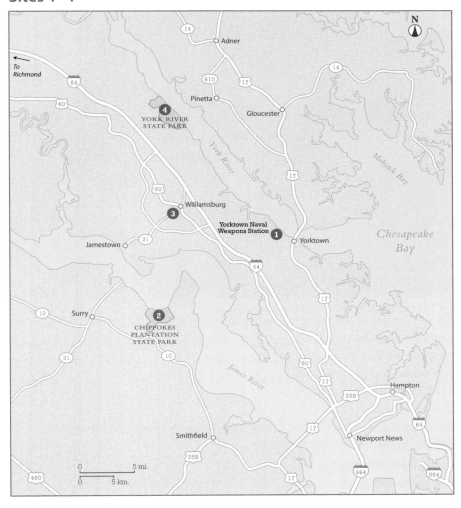

2. Chippokes Plantation State Park Fossils

The cliffs are loaded with fossils but digging is prohibited.

See map page 39.
County: Surry County
Site type: River Shoreline
Land status: Virginia State Park
Material: Fossils
Host rock: Lower Pleistocene Charles City Formation sand, gravel, and clay.
Difficulty: Easy
Family-friendly: Yes
Tools needed: None
Special concerns: No digging allowed in cliffs
Special attractions: Chippokes Plantation Mansion and Grounds
GPS parking: N37°08′46″ / W76°44′22″
GPS Fossil Cliffs: N37°08′46″ / W76°44′15″

Fossil scallops, barnacles, oysters, corals, and shark teeth can be found on the shoreline.

Topographic quadrangle: Surry, VA
Finding the site: The address of Chippokes State Park is 695 Chippokes ParkRd., Surry, VA 23883. From I-95 and I-295, take VA-10 toward Hopewell. Follow VA-10 east for approximately 40 miles to Surry. From Surry, turn left (east) at the intersection of VA-10 and VA-31, and continue on VA-10 for 1.8 miles. Turn left (northeast) on to VA-634, which is Alliance Road. Proceed 3.6 miles, and turn left (northeast) onto VA-655. Continue from here to the parking area in the State Park. Because of weight restrictions, those heading east in vehicles weighing more than 3 tons should avoid taking Highgate Road off VA-10.

Rockhounding

Chippokes Plantation, now a Virginia State Park, has been a working farm since 1619. It is among the oldest continually farmed plantations in the country. It is on the South Bank of the James River and fossils are found along a long stretch of the shoreline.

Start at the visitor center next to the parking lot and get a park map. The Center has many examples of the fossils that can be found in the park. The

State Fossil of Virginia, *Chesapecten Jeffersonius*, is a common fossil along the shoreline and can easily be found in the park. *Chesapecten* is an extinct scallop. Native Americans found they made good scraping tools and bowls. The fossil was named for Thomas Jefferson in 1824, and became the Virginia

This large intact scallop fossils was found on the beach.

State Fossil in 1993. The center has large specimens of this fossil as well as shark teeth, barnacles, and other fossils, and warns visitors to be careful of the sharp edges of the fossils.

Walk down to the beach, and you will see that the shoreline is littered with many pieces of broken fossils. We continued east to the edge of the Park border at Lower Chippokes Creek and the banks at this location have abundant fossil shells, but most of them are small and broken. We later hiked west back along the shoreline and reached the cliffs that are on the west side of the park along the shoreline. The cliffs are sandy sediments and have bedded sections that are nearly entirely fossils. Many large specimens of *Chesapecten*, barnacles, and other fossils are exposed in the cliffs. The cliffs have a sign that says "Restricted Area-No Trespassing" so I made sure to stay out of this area. Digging is prohibited in the cliffs, so I looked for loose fossils on the shoreline. Several large intact shells can be found in this area, and we also found some shark teeth. The best fossils are found in this area as they have not been as subject to erosion and wave action as the fossils further to the east. This would be an excellent place to visit after a hurricane or other large storm exposes more of these fossil-bearing cliffs.

Reference: USGS, 2005

3. Lake Matoaka Spillway Fossils

This large *Chesapecten Jeffersonius* was carefully extracted from the outcrop.

See map page 39.
County/City: Williamsburg City
Site type: Stream bank in spillway below dam
Land status: College of William and Mary. Not posted against trespassing.
Material: Fossils
Host rock: Lower Pleistocene/Upper Pliocene Windsor Formation sand, gravel, and clay
Difficulty: Easy
Family-friendly: Yes
Tools needed: Hammer with pick end, gloves
Special concerns: Parking restricted in the area. Collecting status uncertain
Special attractions: Colonial Williamsburg
GPS parking*: N37°15'52" / W76°43'10"
* *Note*: Parking in this area may be restricted, visitors may consider other parking areas.
GPS Spillway fossils: N37°15'48" / W76°43'20"

The outcrop below the spillway is small but loaded with fossils.

Topographic quadrangle: Williamsburg, VA
Finding the site: From I-64, take VA-199 south for 9.4 miles to VA-5. Turn left (northeast) on VA-5, which is Jamestown Road and proceed 0.8 mile to the dam site. The fossil bearing rocks are on the southeast side of the creek below the dam, which is crossed by Jamestown Road. Parking is restricted in the area as this is a college campus. I parked on an early Saturday evening on Rolfe Road, which is just east of the dam. However, there were signs indicating that I needed a parking sticker. I was there for a short time and did not get a ticket, but you must be aware that it may be difficult to find nonrestricted parking. Colleges are notorious for a lack of parking.

Rockhounding

Lake Matoaka is named after Chief Powhatan's daughter Matoaka, who is better known as Pocahontas. The lake is a 40-acre man-made lake on the campus of the College of William and Mary. The lake was constructed by English colonists around 1718, making it the oldest man-made lake in Virginia and one of the oldest in the Americas.

In the late 1980s, chronic sewage spills and elevated pathogenic bacteria levels forced lake closure to the public. Although the sewage leaks were soon

The fossil outcrops in the banks that are just visible south and east of the spillway.

fixed and bacteria levels returned to normal low levels within a year, the lake remains closed to public use, and fishing and swimming are prohibited. However, the lake is surrounded by trails and the trails are open for hiking.

On the east side of the spillway, below the dam, is a small fossil outcrop that has some of the largest fossils that I have seen in Virginia. I visited the area in late summer. A small trail leads from the sidewalk down to the east bank of College Creek. I immediately saw several large broken fossil shells. Many of the fossils were pieces of *Chesapecten jeffersonius*. I also noticed a horrible smell that seemed to be a combination of dead fish and shellfish, which indicated that the water below the dam is likely polluted. I wore gloves and boots and avoided contact with the water as much as I could.

The best fossils are in the outcrop. The edges of many shells are exposed and they can be carefully dug out with the pick end of a rock hammer. I found the biggest intact *Chesapecten* that I have ever collected at this site. The fossils are extremely fragile and you must be careful not to break them. This is another site that should be visited after flood events or severe rainstorms that expose more shells.

Reference: USGS, 2005

4. York River State Park Fossils

The beach is full of driftwood, and fossils can be found along the shoreline.

See map page 39.
County: James City
Site type: Loose fossils on streambank
Land status: Virginia State Park
Material: Fossils
Host rock: Miocene Eastover and Pliocene Yorktown Formation
Difficulty: Easy
Family-friendly: Yes
Tools needed: None
Special concerns: Permission or a permit from park officials is needed to collect fossils, fossil collecting reportedly frowned upon
Special attractions: Busch Gardens Williamsburg, historic Jamestowne
GPS parking: N37°24'50" / W76°42'50"
GPS Fossil Beach: N37°24'38" / W76°42'18"
Topographic quadrangle: Gressitt, VA

The Virginia State Fossil, *Chesapecten Jeffersonius*, is common at this site.

Finding the site: The address of the park is 9801 York River Park Rd., Williamsburg, VA 23188. From I-64, take the Croaker exit 231B. Go north on Rte. 607, which is Croaker Road, for approximately 1.0 mile. Turn right (east) on Rte. 606, which is Riverview Road. Continue about 1.5 miles to the park entrance. Take a left turn into the Park. From the parking lot you can follow the trail to Fossil Beach, which is about 0.5 mile east. It is strongly suggested that you download a trail map of the park prior to your visit.

Rockhounding

Any place named Fossil Beach is worth exploring. This is a fantastic place for fossils. During our trip to York River State Park, we arrived very late in the day due to traffic. Unfortunately the park was soon going to close. We paid our entrance fee in the drop box but I was concerned that we might not get out in time before the park closed. There were still several picnickers so I thought we had enough time to get to Fossil Beach.

You have to walk about 0.5 mile to Fossil Beach from the parking area, and the trail map is helpful so you do not take a wrong trail. We arrived at Fossil Beach with plenty of daylight to look for fossils.

The base of these cliffs along the York River are thick with fossils, but digging in the cliffs is prohibited.

The site has many large fossils. The most striking are the large scallop shells of *Chesapecten jeffersonius*. Large fossil barnacles are common and are often attached to the scallops. These large fossils are found loose on the beach. The cliffs are full of smaller fossils, including turritella shells, but digging into the cliffs is prohibited. I hoped we would find shark teeth, but we did not find any. The large scallop and barnacle fossils more than make up for the lack of shark teeth.

References: Hobbs, 2009; Say, 1824

5. Westmoreland State Park Shark Teeth

Westmoreland State Park beach is next to large cliffs that constantly erode and drop more shark teeth into the surf.

County/City: Westmoreland County
Site type: Beach
Land status: Westmoreland State Park
Material: Shark teeth
Host rock: Beach sediments, weathered from Miocene Choptank Formation
Difficulty: Easy to moderate
Family-friendly: Yes
Tools needed: None, digging prohibited
Special concerns: Must stay away from cliffs
Special attractions: Impressive shark teeth display in the visitor center
GPS parking: N38°10'11" / W76°51'49"
GPS Fossil Beach: N38°10'01" / W76°51'16"

This large tooth was picked up on the beach and was one of the largest teeth that we saw at this beach.

Topographic quadrangle: Stratford Hall, VA-MD
Finding the site: From US-301, turn left onto VA-3 E. Go 17.7 miles and turn left onto VA-347 N to enter Westmoreland State Park. Go 1.8 miles and turn right onto SR 686. Go 0.2 mile and park at the visitor center parking lot. From here, you can hike a little over a ½ mile on the Big Meadow Trail to Fossil Beach, which is the main beach for hikers to collect shark teeth in the park. Note that this is a different fossil beach than the one described in Site 4.

Rockhounding

This is a well-known beach for shark teeth in Virginia. The shark teeth are from extinct Miocene sharks and are from sediments of the Choptank Formation of the Chesapeake Group. The visitor center has a great display of shark teeth, but it is important to remember that these were collected over decades and long before the beach was known for collecting shark teeth.

We arrived on a rainy June morning, so we did not have a lot of competition from other collectors. We were among the first people on the beach but

This display of shark teeth in the visitor center shows teeth from the early years of collecting at the beach.

more showed up as the weather began to improve slightly. We first used a small screen to sift through the sand and gravel of the shoreline, but soon focused on just looking for teeth at the water's edge without a screen. We were able to find only small teeth, but a young boy found a large tooth that appeared to be from a goblin shark, and a lady with her family found a very large tooth just walking along the beach. The teeth are there, but it takes patience and luck to find them.

References: Ward and Blackwelder, 1975; Frye, 1986

Sites 5–9

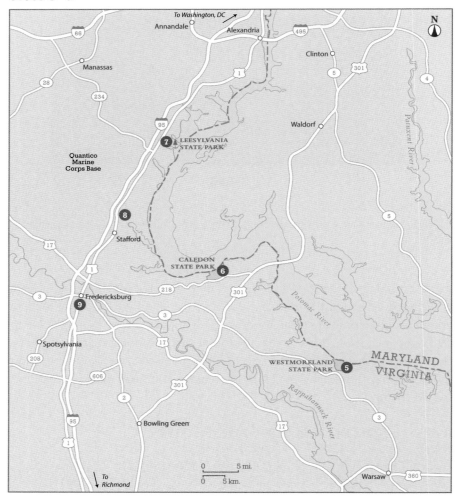

6. Caledon State Park Shark Teeth

The teeth that we found at this beach were much larger than those at many other beaches.

See map page 52.
County: King George County
Site type: Beach
Land status: Caledon State Park
Material: Shark teeth
Host rock: Beach sediments
Difficulty: Easy
Family-friendly: Yes
Tools needed: None, but a small shovel/screen may be useful
Special concerns: Moderate hike to beach
Special attractions: Solitude, fishing on the Potomac River
GPS parking: N38°20'02" / W77°08'35"
GPS beach: N38°20'55" / W77°09'28"
Topographic quadrangle: King George, VA-MD

Watching the waves wash teeth onto the beach still seems the best way to find shark teeth.

Finding the site: From I-95, take exit 133 A and merge onto US 17 S. Go 2.1 miles, and this turns into VA-218 E. Follow this for 20.2 miles, and turn a slight left (north) into the road for the park. Continue to the right for 0.2 mile and park in the parking lot near the buildings. The trailhead to go to the beach, which is the Boyd's Hole Trail, is directly to the north. On the way to the beach, you will encounter an area known as the Triangle. Stay on the Boyd's Hole Trail, which is the right fork at the triangle, and you will soon reach the beach. The total hike is approximately 1.25 miles.

Rockhounding

This is a very long and secluded beach that has large shark teeth. We came to the site as the tide was coming in, and we were able to find several teeth by walking along the shore and simply looking down where the waves met the shoreline. Some of these were much larger than we had found at Westmoreland Beach, Virginia, and nearby Purse State Park in Maryland. The area of the beach does not have any significant cliffs. We attempted to

A walk on the beach can offer both shark teeth and solitude, depending when you visit.

walk to some small cliffs upstream and to the west but were soon stopped by both the cliffs and the signs stating we would be entering private land. The beach is loaded with driftwood, but fortunately most of this wood is away from the beach so it is easy to walk along the shoreline without climbing or tripping over logs. While collecting shark teeth is allowed, driftwood collecting is not.

Reference: Virginia Department of Mineral Resources, 2003

7. Leesylvania State Park Sandstone

The sandstone is coarse and has some minor limonite bands.

See map page 52.
County/City: Prince William County
Site type: Former quarry
Land status: Virginia State Park
Material: Sandstone
Host rock: Lower Cretaceous Potomac Group Sandstone
Difficulty: Easy
Family-friendly: Yes
Tools needed: None
Special concerns: State Park, no collecting allowed
Special attractions: Fishing pier at Leesylvania State Park
GPS parking: N38°35′26″ / W77°14′59″
GPS Freestone Point Quarry: N38°35′32″ / W77°14′47″

Sandstone cliffs are visible from the Fishing Pier, but access to the base of the cliffs is blocked to visitors from the beach.

Topographic quadrangle: Indian Head, MD-VA
Finding the site: The address of the park is 2001 Daniel K. Ludwig Dr., Woodbridge, VA 22191-4504. From I-95, take Rippon Landing exit 156, then go east on Dale Boulevard to US-1, which is Jefferson Davis Highway. Proceed approximately 1 mile on US-1, and turn left (east) on to Neabsco Road. Continue on this road and turn left onto Daniel K. Ludwig Drive. Follow this road into the park. It is strongly suggested that you download a trail map of the park prior to your visit.

Rockhounding

Freestone Point, located at the northeast end of Leesylvania State Park, was the site of a sandstone quarry in the late 1700s and early 1800s. The sandstone was easy to quarry and this resulted in the name "Freestone." Mixon et al. (1972) refer to the strata exposed at Freestone Point as the Lower Cretaceous Potomac Group. This sandstone was used as building material for many houses and public buildings, but it was soft and not durable. Better sources of building stone were soon found elsewhere.

This large block of sandstone is along the cliffside and is representative of the sandstone extracted from the quarry.

During the Civil War a battery with four individual gun emplacements was installed on the cliffs of Freestone Point. The battery was used to help blockade the Potomac River from October 1861 to March 1862. However, the Freestone Point battery could never control that part of the Potomac, and Union ships soon learned to stay out of its range. It was abandoned after other larger batteries were built, but the basic earthen mounds and depressions from the batteries remained, and they are now equipped with period artillery pieces.

The Freestone Point area gets hundreds of visitors including picnickers and fisherman. The sandstone can still be seen along the sides of the cliffs near the point. Access to the base of the cliffs is blocked to visitors coming from the beach, and I did not get to check access from the trails that lead to the point near the top of the cliffs. Ironically, while fossil collecting is allowed in many state parks, rock collecting is not, so you are not supposed to collect at this locality. It is still a worthwhile site to visit.

The sandstone is generally coarse and off-white. Some sections have limonite banding. The sandstone is soft and is easy to break apart. The sandstone is also reported to have blue quartz, but I did not see any. The blue quartz source may be from the late Precambrian rocks of the Blue Ridge Province in Virginia, as blue quartz is common in these rocks.

References: Mixon et al., 1972; National Park Service, 1989

8. Government Island Sandstone Quarry

The cuts made to carve the sandstone nearly 200 years ago are still prominent.

See map page 52.
County/City: Stafford County
Site type: Former sandstone quarry
Land status: Stafford County Parks and Recreation
Material: Brown sandstone
Host rock: Cretaceous Aquia Creek Formation
Difficulty: Easy
Family-friendly: Yes
Tools needed: None
Special concerns: County park, no collecting allowed, strictly for observation only
Special attractions: Several local Civil War sites
GPS parking: N38°26'48.9" / W77°23'18"
GPS quarry area: N38°26'59" / W77°22'48"

The main quarry area is watched by a security camera.

Topographic quadrangle: Stafford, VA
Finding the site: From I-95 north, take exit 140 for CR 630. Go 0.2 mile and turn right (east) onto Courthouse Road. Go 0.7 mile and turn left (north) onto US-1 N. Go 1.7 miles and turn right (east) onto Coal Landing Road. Go 0.7 mile and look for the parking area to your left (north). From here you can follow the trail to Governor Island and the former quarry. The address for the parking area is 191 Coal Landing Rd., Stafford, VA 22554.

Rockhounding

Government Island Quarry is a former quarry that supplied stone for many buildings in Washington, DC, and the surrounding region. The land for the quarry was bought in 1791 to supply stone for the nation's new capitol in Washington, DC. The quarry was positioned next to the Potomac River, and the stone was loaded on barges and transported to Washington. Washington was still nearly 50 miles away and upstream, so it still must have been quite a task to get the stone to the capital. The buildings that incorporate the stone into their construction include the White House, the US Capitol, and the US Treasury.

The Cretaceous Aquia Creek Sandstone is known as "freestone," as it is a fine-grained stone that can be easily cut in any direction without splitting. However, it was a terrible building stone. Despite the relatively consistent grain size, the stone had lumps of clay and occasional large pebbles, and some sections were poorly cemented. By the early 1800s the limitations of the stone were obvious, and the last use of the stone for buildings was in 1827. In 1849, the head of the building committee for the Smithsonian Institution said that

The sharp cuts in the sandstone are still visible and the quarry now has many large trees.

he would not want the stone even if it were free. The quarry soon fell into disuse and was abandoned. In the late twentieth century the historic significance of the site was recognized, and in 2009 the former quarry was established as a county park with trails and interpretative signs. The quarry has a trail that circles Governor Island, and from the parking lot is a 1.5-mile walk. The area is also an ideal location to see plants, birds, and wildlife, and many people also fish in Aquia Creek in the park. The quarry was also featured on the History Channel on November 9, 2013, in *10 Things You Don't Know About: The White House.* I caught this show just by chance in late 2013 and made a promise to myself to find and visit this quarry.

The Cretaceous Aquia Creek Sandstone should not be confused with the Paleocene Aquia Formation, as the Aquia Formation is very soft as it is made of glauconitic sand and clay. When we visited the area we were able to walk around the entire island and visit some of the former quarried areas. The Aquia Creek Sandstone is consistently brown and fine-to-medium grained, and you can see some of the differential weathering that ultimately made it a poor material for building. The county is apparently very serious about no collecting at this site, as a security camera is positioned in the main quarry area. This is the part of the island that almost certainly gets the most visitors. Assuming it is a motion-activated camera, it must be a real challenge to manage all of the resulting image and video data for this quarry.

References: Free Lance Star, 1992; USGS, 1998

9. Alum Spring Park Wood Fossils

The sandstone cliff in the park is a prominent feature and is full of wood fossil casts.

See map page 52.
County/City: City of Fredericksburg
Site type: Sandstone Cliffs and talus
Land status: City Park
Material: Wood fossils
Host rock: Lower Cretaceous Patuxent arkose
Difficulty: Easy
Family-friendly: Yes
Tools needed: None
Special concerns: Collecting is not allowed as it is a city park. Must also be careful on cliffs, especially with small children
Special attractions: Fredericksburg Battlefield
GPS parking: N38°17'20" / W77°28'54"
GPS Sandstone Cliff: N38°17'17"N / W77°29'01"
Topographic quadrangle: Fredericksburg, VA

Loose rocks with fragments of fossil wood are found below the cliffs near the creek.

Finding the site: From I-95, take exit 130A and proceed east on Plank Road/SR 3 E for approximately 1.7 miles. This soon turns into Williams Street, also known as the Blue and Gray Parkway further east. Turn right (south) onto Greenbriar Drive and follow this to the end of the road. You will enter Alum Spring Park. Drive through Hazel Run, and the parking lot is at the end of Greenbrier Drive. The sandstone cliff can be reached by trails and it is approximately 700 feet west of the parking lot.

Rockhounding

This is an outstanding site to see fossil wood in sandstone. Alum Spring Park is a city park that offers free admission, and when I visited the park on a Saturday afternoon in September 2016, it was full of families and picnickers. The trails are generally level and there are some sections with steps to reach elevated areas in the park. The sandstone cliffs are due west of the parking area and I found them by hiking along the trails in an upstream direction along Hazel Run.

The cliffs are a prominent feature of the park. They were reportedly used for shelter by civilians during the bombardment of Fredericksburg in 1862.

The cliffs reportedly provided shelter during the bombardment of Fredericksburg in the Civil War.

The fossil wood can be seen as pieces and casts within Lower Cretaceous arkose of the Patuxent Formation, which forms the cliffs. The Patuxent Formation is the basal unit of the Coastal Plain sediments and unconformably overlies the crystalline basement. This unconformity is the subsurface equivalent of the

Fall line, which marks the break between the soft sediments of the Coastal Plain and the hard crystalline rocks of the Piedmont.

A sign near the parking area describes the cliffs and states that fossil wood should not be collected from the cliffs. However, the sign also says that specimens may be collected along the bed of the former railway that crossed the park. I found an abundance of hand samples with wood casts and wood fragments below the cliffs. I looked along the former railroad bed above the cliffs, but did not see any fossil wood in this area, despite the loose arkosic exposures along the rail cut. The sandstone cliff and the talus below the cliff offer the best area to see the fossil wood.

The area reportedly has small concretions of pyrite, but I did not see any in the outcrops on the cliff or in the talus on the ground. I also looked briefly in the stream for any interesting rocks, but the stream gravels appeared to be quartz and weathered feldspar, typical of sediments in Coastal Plain streams. Although called the Alum Spring Park because it reportedly produced alum, I did not see any alum in any of the rocks.

While you cannot distinguish this with the naked eye, the quartz in the fossil wood has been identified as tridymite. This is a high-temperature form of quartz, and it is very unusual to find tridymite in rocks that most likely formed at low temperatures.

Reference: Mitchell, 1967

PIEDMONT

10. Windy Run Quartz and Schorl

The waterfall at Windy Run is a trickle in the summer but is undoubtedly much larger during the spring and during flood events.

County: Arlington

Site type: Loose rocks in stream bed

Land status: Windy Run Park

Material: White quartz and black tourmaline, known as schorl

Host rock: Precambrian granitic and metamorphic rocks

Difficulty: Hard

Family-friendly: Yes

Tools needed: Hammer, if you wish to break any rocks

Special concerns: Trail becomes steep near the Potomac River. Site is also in Windy Run Park, which does not allow rock collecting

Special attractions: Washington, DC

GPS parking: N38°54'09" / W77°05'55"

GPS Schorl Area: N38°54'21"N / W77°05'37

Topographic quadrangle: Washington West, DC MD VA

Finding the site: From I-66 East, take exit 72 for US-29/Lee Highway toward Spout Run Parkway. Turn left (west) and go approximately 0.3 mile on Hwy. 29. Turn right (north) on North Lincoln Street, go about 0.1 mile. Turn left (west) onto 21 Ave. north. Turn right again on to North Lincoln Street, and then turn left on 23 Ave. North. This soon becomes North Monroe Street. Continue about 0.1 mile and turn right on Lorcom Lane. Go about 0.1 mile and turn left onto north Kenmore Street. Proceed about 0.2 mile to the parking area. Park here, and hike down a trail to the Potomac River. The schorl can be found around the base of the waterfall where Windy Run enters the Potomac.

Rockhounding

This is a scenic site and has abundant quartz, but the schorl is extremely difficult to find. To find the schorl you have to find the white quartz that formed as pegmatite quartz as opposed to smaller secondary vein quartz. You then have to break apart the quartz to find the black tourmaline. Much of the quartz at this site is barren, and it is easy to mistake white quartzite for pegmatite quartz until you break it apart. The white quartzite will have a sandy

The schorl is hard to find but the black crystals are easy to see in the white quartz.

The base of the waterfall is full of gray metamorphic rocks and you have to look for the white quartz to find the schorl.

appearance and will often have some light orange iron staining. The quartz rocks that you break apart that are a solid bright white are your best opportunities of finding the schorl.

I had nearly given up when I found a large bright white boulder about 2 feet wide. I broke it apart, which took considerable effort, and I found black radiating crystals of tourmaline. They were quite small but I was pleased that I was eventually able to find the schorl at this site. The waterfall and the view of the Potomac by themselves make this a great site to visit, and the black tourmaline is really just a bonus.

Reference: Bernstein, 1980

Sites 10–14

11. Turkey Run Steatite and Sillimanite

Turkey Run has a flat area west of the parkway bridge and the vegetation is thick in some sections.

See map page 71.
County: Fairfax
Site type: Loose rocks in stream bed
Land status: National Park Service
Material: Steatite and sillimanite
Host rock: Precambrian granitic and metamorphic rocks
Difficulty: Hard
Family-friendly: Yes
Tools needed: Hammer, but note restrictions on rock collecting
Special concerns: Area is controlled by National Park Service, collecting not allowed

Breaking apart the gneiss in the streambed can reveal sections with radiating sillimanite crystals.

Special attractions: Great Falls National Park
GPS parking: N38°57'51" / W77°09'11"
GPS Turkey Run: N38°54'21" / W77°05'37"
Topographic quadrangle: Falls Church, VA-MD
Finding the site: From I-495, take exit 43 south to the George Washington Memorial Parkway. Continue 1.4 miles and take the exit for Turkey Run Park. The road will cross back over the parkway. Take the first left, which is the Turkey Run Loop Road, and park at the parking lot just northeast of the Turkey Run Loop Road. From here you can follow the trail to Turkey Run.

Rockhounding
Turkey Run is a ravine that cuts through Precambrian metamorphic rocks as it drains into the Potomac. The area is managed by the National Park Service and excellent parking and trails are available to hike into Turkey Run. The ravine is steepest near the river but flattens when it reaches the river flood plain.

The Potomac River is shallow and scenic where Turkey Run enters the river.

A trail along the north side of Turkey Run leads westward, and you can hike beneath the George Washington Memorial Parkway. West of the parkway the drainage does not have as many steep walls. I found the best steatite in boulders upstream of the bridge, but you can find steatite elsewhere as loose rocks in the gorge. The steatite is generally well foliated and rich in chlorite. Most of the rocks in the gorge have some chlorite but in general they are very hard and better described as fine-grained dark gray to green metamorphic rocks.

Radiating sillimanite crystals are present within some of the gneisses in the ravine, and these are best seen on freshly broken surfaces. I found a very nice piece of coarse gneiss with abundant sillimanite crystals near the area where Turkey Run meets the Potomac River. Bernstein (1980) did not specifically mention steatite at this location, but noted that Reed and Jolly (1963) said that sillimanite needles up to 2.5 centimeters long, often in fan- or sheath-like aggregates, constitutes up to 20 percent of some of the schists along the

Potomac River between Great Falls and Turkey Island, both of which are upstream from this locality. The gneiss that I found with the sillimanite likely washed downstream from the Great Falls/Turkey Island area. The sillimanite-bearing gneisses are not common at Turkey Run, but you may get lucky if you keep your eyes open. The ravine and the Potomac River make this an excellent site even without the steatite or sillimanite.

References: Bernstein, 1980; Reed and Jolly, 1963

12. Great Falls of the Potomac Gneiss

The Great Falls of the Potomac is a spectacular feature of the Piedmont Province.

See map page 71.
County/City: Fairfax
Site type: Outcrops on Potomac River
Land status: National Park Service
Material: Banded and migmatitic gneiss
Host rock: Precambrian Mather Gorge Formation Metagraywacke
Difficulty: Easy
Family-friendly: Yes
Tools needed: None.
Special concerns: Area is controlled by National Park Service, collecting not allowed. Must also be extremely careful near cliffs and river
Special attractions: Washington, DC
GPS parking: N38°59'53" / W77°15'20"

Beautiful migmatitic gneiss is prominent along the trails south of the main falls.

GPS Overlook: N38°59′47″ / W77°15′12″
Topographic quadrangle: Vienna, VA-MD
Finding the site: The address of the Park is 9200 Old Dominion Drive, McLean, VA 22102. From I-495, take exit 44 to VA-193. Continue on north on VA-193 for 4.2 miles. Turn right (north) onto Old Dominion Drive and proceed 1.1 miles to the parking lot. You will also have to pay a fee to enter the park prior to reaching the parking area. From here, proceed to the visitor center and follow the trails to the overlooks.

Rockhounding

While this is not a site for collecting rocks, the Great Falls of the Potomac should be visited when you are in the Washington, DC, area. The Great Falls are considered by many to be the most impressive natural feature in the region. The Potomac is usually a wide, flat river, but as it approaches the Fall Line between the Piedmont and Coastal Plain sediments, the river is constricted and picks up speed. The river narrows from nearly 1,000 feet wide, just above the falls, to between 60 and 100 feet wide as it rushes through Mather Gorge, a short distance below the falls. It cuts deeply into the metamorphic bedrock and forms a series of steep rapids and waterfalls. The falls consist of cascading rapids and several 20-feet waterfalls, with a total 76-feet drop in elevation in less than a mile. The Great Falls of the Potomac display the steepest and most impressive Fall Line rapids of the eastern rivers.

Downstream of the Visitor Center the banks become extremely steep.

The rocks are mapped as late Precambrian metagraywacke of the Glen Arm Series, which is interbedded with schist. This tough, erosion-resistant metamorphic rock is well jointed and the river follows joint patterns. Excellent examples of banded and migmatitic gneiss can be seen throughout the gorge.

The trails are well established at the park. The gneissic rocks are well exposed at the outlooks and on the trails south of the Great Falls along the west side of Mather Gorge, which is a remarkably straight section of the Potomac River. The area receives thousands of visitors, and many kayakers and rafters can also been seen in Mather Gorge.

Reference: USGS, 2005

13. Leesburg Potomac Marble

The outcrops with Potomac Marble are easy to see from the road.

See map page 71.

County/City: Loudoun

Site type: Roadcut with loose rocks

Land status: Highway right-of-way, not posted

Material: Potomac marble

Host rock: Leesburg Limestone Conglomeratic member of the Bull Run Formation

Difficulty: Easy

Family-friendly: Yes

Tools needed: None

Special concerns: Traffic can be become busy along Rte. 15

Special attractions: Ida Lee Park, City of Leesburg

GPS parking: N39°07'52" / N77°05'55"

Topographic quadrangle: Waterford, VA-MD

Potomac marble is colorful but its decorative features made it a terrible building stone.

Finding the site: From Leesburg, proceed north on US Business 15/North King Street approximately 1.3 miles. The outcrops of Potomac Marble are on the right (east) side of the road. The parking area is a small section on the west side of the road. This is south of the roadcut and it is wide enough for safe parking.

Rockhounding

This is an easily accessed roadcut with exposures of colorful Potomac marble. Potomac marble is sometimes referred to as "calico rock" or "Potomac breccia." Potomac marble is the Leesburg Limestone Conglomeratic member of the Bull Run Formation and is Triassic in age. The Leesburg member is a distinct carbonate conglomerate with subangular to subrounded pebbles, cobbles, and boulders of limestone and dolomite in a reddish-brown silty matrix. The carbonate clasts are likely from the Cambrian–Early Paleozoic age Frederick Limestone and Tomstown Formations, which are exposed in the region of Furnace Mountain, Virginia, and north of the Potomac River in Frederick County, Maryland.

The conglomerate formed from debris flows on alluvial fans. Potomac marble was quarried and used for the columns in Statuary Hall in the Capitol

The Potomac marble is adbundant and the biggest challenge is picking out the best pieces from so many rocks.

in Washington, DC. While the stone has a beautiful pattern, it has many features that make it a terrible building stone. It varies in texture, clasts fall out, and when used outside, it is subject to differential weathering of the limestone, dolomite, and matrix. Building engineers soon came to their senses and stopped using the rock as an exterior building stone.

The parking area is just south of the outcrops. The parking is on the west side of the road, and the outcrops are on the east side. I highly recommend wearing a high-visibility vest in this area. The outcrops are well off the road but you want to make sure you are visible to traffic. Many of the rocks are loose, and a hammer is only needed to trim pieces and expose fresh surfaces. Potomac marble is also exposed as rounded knobs in nearby Leesburg Park, but collecting in the park is prohibited. This roadcut offers an excellent opportunity to see Potomac marble and the exposures are far better than those in the park, as the rock has been broken apart and exposed by road construction.

References: Beard, 2015; Kuff and Brooks, 2007; Southworth et al., 1999; Withington, 1975

14. Evergreen Mills Banded Metasediments

The banded rocks are hard but fractured and are easy to break off the outcrop beneath the bridge.

See map page 71.
County: Loudoun
Site type: Outcrops under bridge
Land status: Uncertain, likely private, but not posted
Material: Banded contact metamorphic rocks
Host rock: Upper Triassic Newark Supergroup Sediments
Difficulty: Easy
Family-friendly: No, climb to outcrops is steep and not for everyone
Tools needed: Hammer and chisel
Special concerns: Steep climb to outcrops
Special attractions: None

The banded rocks are exposed beneath the bridge on the south side of Goose Creek.

GPS parking: N39°01'03.0" / W77°34'37.0"
GPS banded metamorphics: N39°01'06" / W77°34'38"
Topographic quadrangle: Leesburg, VA-MD
Finding the site: From Leesburg, take South King Street, which is US-15, south and turn left (east) onto Evergreen Mills Road. Proceed 6.0 miles and turn right (west) onto VA-860, which is Watson Road. The parking area is approximately 250 feet from the intersection of VA-860 and Watson Road, and is on the right (north) side of the road.

Rockhounding

This site reportedly has garnet and other contact metamorphic minerals exposed in roadcuts near the intersection of Evergreen Mills Road and Watson Road near Goose Creek. While rocks are exposed in this area, I did not find any significant minerals adjacent to the roads. However, an interesting section of banded metasediments is exposed beneath the south side of the bridge where it crosses Goose Creek.

The climb under the bridge is tricky and you must be careful as the rocks are often loose.

These rocks are contact metamorphosed sandstones and shales of the Triassic Newark Supergroup, and much of the original bedding is retained in the rocks. The sediments were metamorphosed from the heat and pressure from the massive Jurassic diabase intrusions just east of this area.

The metamorphism combined with the original bedding gives the rocks a distinct banded appearance. The colors range from orange to green. The rocks are fine grained, and I did not see any individual garnet crystals, but the banding and colors make up for the lack of coarse-grained minerals. The rocks are also relatively easy to split off the outcrop with a hammer and are much easier to break off if you come equipped with a chisel.

References: Bernstein, 1980; USGS, 2005

15. Hadensville Metapyroxenite

The metapyroxenite outcrop can be spotted by the dark rocks on the sides of the road.

County/City: Goochland County
Site type: Roadcut
Land status: Private, but roadcut is not posted
Material: Pyroxenite
Host rock: Cambrian Ta River Metamorphic Suite, amphibolite, and gneiss
Difficulty: Easy
Family-friendly: Yes
Tools needed: Hammer
Special concerns: Parking is adequate but the road has high traffic
Special attractions: Lake Anna State Park
GPS parking: N37°51'03" / W78°00'19"
Topographic quadrangle: Caledonia, VA

Finding the site: From I-64, take exit 152 to VA 629 west. Continue 0.6 mile and turn right (northwest) on to US 250 west. Proceed 0.9 mile and look for a road cut on a low hill. Park in the limited parking on the east side of the road. The pyroxenite is on both sides of the road.

Rockhounding

Like many roadcuts in the Piedmont, this site can easily be missed. According to Spears et al. (2004) this roadcut exposes one of the most prominent mafic to ultramafic dike-like bodies in the Piedmont Province of Virginia. It is described as a metapyroxenite, which is a metamorphosed ultramafic igneous rock comprised of minerals of the pyroxene group. Pyroxenite is a deep dark green to black rock and sometimes has well-formed minerals, especially in coarse-grained sections.

When I was looking for this site, I drove by it at first, but then realized that there were some large dark-green to black rocks exposed on the south side of US 250. I was able to find a small area to pull over on the east side of the road. I am certain that this is the locality reference in Spears et al. (2004).

Weathered surfaces reveal knobs of pyroxene in the metapyroxenite.

When broken, the tiny cleavage planes of the pyroxene give the rock a sparkling appearance.

The metapyroxenite is exposed in the roadcut and several small loose pieces can be found next to the road and on the slopes of the roadcut. I broke several pieces and found that some of them had unweathered pyroxenes and what appeared to be abundant dark green chlorite. The rock sparkles in bright sunlight as the sun reflects off the cleavage planes of the pyroxenes and chlorite. Weathering helps expose some of the pyroxenes on unbroken surfaces, and the surfaces of the coarse-grained rocks are rough with innumerable small knobs of pyroxenes.

This is one of the better roadcut exposures I have seen in the Virginia Piedmont. The surrounding area is still relatively flat, and roadcuts with bedrock exposures can be hard to find, especially cuts with the more unusual rocks.

References: Spears et al., 2004; USGS, 2005

Sites 15–17

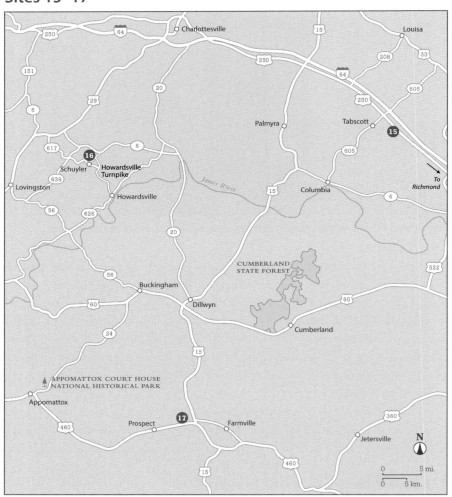

Charlottesville · Louisa · 250 · 64 · 15 · 250 · 208 · 33 · 151 · 20 · 64 · 250 · 608 · 29 · 6 · 617 · Palmyra · Tabscott · **15** · 16 · 6 · 808 · **To Richmond** · Schuyler · Howardsville Turnpike · James River · 639 · Howardsville · 15 · Columbia · 6 · Lovingston · 56 · 626 · 20 · CUMBERLAND STATE FOREST · 522 · 56 · Buckingham · 80 · 60 · Dillwyn · 24 · Cumberland · 15 · APPOMATTOX COURT HOUSE NATIONAL HISTORICAL PARK · 360 · Appomattox · **17** · 460 · Prospect · Farmville · Jetersville · **N** · 15 · 460 · 0 5 mi. · 0 5 km.

16. Schuyler Soapstone Quarry

The quarry is full of water and has some graffiti on the sides.

See map page 90.
County/City: Nelson County
Site type: Inactive quarry
Land status: Uncertain. Not posted
Material: Soapstone, aka talc schist
Host rock: Late Precambrian metamorphosed ultramafic rocks
Difficulty: Easy
Family-friendly: Yes
Tools needed: Hammer
Special concerns: Quarry is filled with water and the highwalls can be dangerous
Special attractions: Walton's Mountain Museum in Schuyler
GPS parking: N37°47'47" / W78°41'34"
GPS soapstone outcrops at quarry: N37°47'46" / W78°41'37"
Topographic quadrangle: Schuyler, VA
Finding the site: From US-29, take VA-6 5.8 miles east and turn right (south) on Schuyler Road. Continue 1.5 miles south, and look for a long, broad shoulder on the left (east) side of Schuyler Road. Park here, and the quarry is just east of the road near the south side of the shoulder.

The outcrops next to the road are soft and slippery when wet, as would be expected of soapstone.

Rockhounding

The Schuyler area is famous for the production of soapstone, and there are active quarry companies in the area. Old soapstone quarries are found throughout the area, but all are on private land and are not accessible without special permission. However, this quarry is not posted against trespassing. It apparently receives many visitors, but I doubt if these visitors have the slightest interest in soapstone.

The shoulder for parking is well used. The quarry has some recent trash, and I was very surprised to see ropes for climbing some of the highwalls and some new looking rope swings, which were used for swinging into the quarry lake. The place appears to be a local party spot. This is unusual as similar quarries are nearly always fenced and do not allow visitors. I later found several YouTube videos of cliff divers at a Schuyler quarry, but I could not confirm if it was the same quarry.

As the quarry is filled with water and the highwalls are steep, the only rocks that I found accessible next to the road were a large, well-foliated out-crop of talc schist. This material can be scraped with your fingernail. I hit it with my hammer pick to break off a piece, and I was surprised at how easily

While it is easy to see the other side, it is extremely dangerous to walk top on the steep highwalls.

my hammer pick could penetrate the schist. The rock was very soft and it was easy to take out small hand samples while minimizing damage to the outcrop.

The rock was also slippery, so I made sure to be extremely careful at this site. It would be easy to slip and fall off the highwalls or the smaller cliffs, and I limited my exploration of the site to the section adjacent to the road. Soapstone, even though it is not really soap, does become slippery when wet, so be careful if you are climbing the outcrops in the rain.

I later explored some of the other quarries I had previously noted at on Google Maps, but all of them were private. The quarry next to Schuyler Road is your best bet if you want a guarantee that you will see some soapstone when you come to Schuyler.

Schuyler also has the Walton's Mountain Museum. This is a museum inspired by the *Waltons*, a TV show based on the life of the show creator, Earl Hamner Jr., who grew up in Schuyler, Virginia. The show portrayed life in rural Virginia in the 1930s and 1940s. Visitors now probably reminisce about watching the TV show in the 1970s as much as life in the 1930s and 1940s.

References: Penick, 1987; USGS, 2005

17. Scufflin Acres Farms Amethyst

The two silos in the background are a great landmark for the gully with the amethyst.

See map page 90.
County/City: Prince Edward County
Site type: Gully on hillside
Land status: Private, Fee-Collecting Site
Material: Amethyst
Host rock: Cambrian interlayered mafic and felsic metavolcanic rocks, including amphibolite, hornblende-biotite gneiss, and schist.
Difficulty: Easy
Family-friendly: Yes
Tools needed: Hammer and garden tools
Special concerns: Site can become very hot during the summer months, lots of vegetation and potential for ticks
Special attractions: Appomattox Court House National Park
GPS parking: N37°19'06" / W78°29'42"
GPS Gully with Amethyst: N37°19'08" / W78°29'42"

Some of the amethyst is dark purple and is found by breaking apart larger rocks.

Topographic quadrangle: Farmville, PA
Finding the site: The address for this site is 261 Scufflin Acres Ln., Prospect, VA 23960. At the time of book preparation the site was on Facebook, and the phone number was (434) 392-4321. From US-460, take VA-645, which is Simpson Road, north for 0.3 mile, and turn onto Scufflin Acres Lane. Continue for 0.2 mile and turn left. The amethyst is found in a gully that drains northward. Park off the road and south of the gully. Two silos can be seen north of the gully at a small farm, and this is a useful landmark. However, before going to the site, be sure to pay the fee. The fee is collected at the house that is just north of the left turn that takes you to the gully.

Rockhounding

This was the only open fee–collecting site that I found in the Piedmont region. Many of the previous sites referenced in the literature have closed or are not otherwise accessible, and phone calls to owners were not returned. Fortunately, the operator of Scufflin Acres was easily reachable and allowed us to collect at the site late on a summer Saturday afternoon.

The gully is easy to reach and the best amethyst is found directly on the ground.

This site is a small gully where the rocks are well exposed. The best way to find the amethyst is to look for loose crystals on the ground and large pieces of quartz and granite that have washed down the gully. Breaking open these pieces sometimes reveals quartz–rich zones with amethyst.

The amethyst varies considerably throughout the site. Some are a light translucent purple and are best described as amethystine, whereas others are a dark opaque purple. Many of the rocks have terminated white quartz crystals but we did not find any large amethyst pieces with terminated crystal points.

This site would be great to visit after a large thunderstorm or a hurricane, as this would help wash more material in the gully. The operator has expressed interest in getting an excavator to expose more fresh material, but the cost and potential permitting issues make this prohibited at present.

Reference: USGS, 2005

18. Pittsylvania Wayside Park Feldspar and Mica

The large cliff of feldspar and mica is just east of the walking bridge on the north side of Sycamore Creek.

County/City: Pittsylvania County
Site type: Large outcrops on stream bank
Land status: Public park
Material: Feldspar and mica
Host rock: Late Proterozoic–Early Cambrian Feldspathic Metagraywacke
Difficulty: Easy
Family-friendly: Yes
Tools needed: Hammer
Special concerns: Access may be difficult during flooding. Collecting status also uncertain
Special attractions: Leesville Lake

GPS parking: N37°05′26″ / W79°19′21″
GPS eastern outcrop: N37°05′28″ / W79°19′22″
Topographic quadrangle: Altavista, VA
Finding the site: From Lynchburg, take US 29 South for 29.3 miles. Take a sharp left (east) onto US 29 Business North toward Altavista, which is also known as Main Street. Proceed approximately 1.0 mile and turn left (north) just before Sycamore Creek. Follow this to the parking area, which is just south of a bridge that crosses Sycamore Creek. Park here, cross the bridge, and walk east (upstream) about 200 feet to the large mass of feldspar and mica that forms a broad white cliff on the north side of Sycamore Creek.

Rockhounding

This is an excellent site for coarse-grained feldspar and mica. Large pieces of graphic granite, which is a variety of quartz-rich granite with a quartz/feldspar pattern that resembles hieroglyphics, are common at this site. The base of the cliff, which has some small workings, has lots of loose rocks and many of these contain good books of muscovite feldspar. Garnet is also reported at

This mica-rich piece was found in the loose rocks at the base of the cliff.

Large masses of mica among white quartz and feldspar are common in the cliff.

this site but we did not find any. The cliff is loaded with large masses of white feldspar, gray quartz, and large books of muscovite. Most of these cannot easily be broken off, so they remain for future visitors to the site.

While this site is easily accessed and easy to find when you know where to go, we almost missed finding this cliff. We first crossed the bridge and walked on some of the park roads. It is worth noting that many of the roads also had good pieces of mica and feldspar. The key is to make sure that you walk upstream from the bridge and look for the first large white cliff next to Sycamore Creek.

References: Penick, 1987; USGS, 2005

Sites 18–20

19. Leesville Actinolite Schist

Parking is adequate next to the roadcut.

See map page 100.
County/City: Campbell County
Site type: Roadcut
Land status: Private, posted, must stay within highway right-of-way
Material: Extremely foliated fine-grained schist
Host rock: Alligator Back Formation Actinolite Schist
Difficulty: Easy
Family-friendly: Yes
Tools needed: Hammer, strictly for trimming loose rocks
Special concerns: Posted ground, must stay outside of no trespassing signs
Special attractions: Smith Mountain Lake State Park
GPS parking: N37°07'28" / W79°23'42"
Topographic quadrangle: Leesville, VA
Finding the site: From the intersection Chellis Ford Road (Rte. 630) and Virginia 43 in Leesville, proceed 0.8 mile west. The roadcut will be on the right (east) side of VA-43. Parking is adequate next to the roadcut, which is easy to see from the road.

The actinolite schist forms elongated rocks that resemble pieces of wood.

Rockhounding

In all my decades of rock collecting, this is one of the strangest outcrops I have encountered. Based on the information from Penick (1987), I thought this roadcut would contain chromian muscovite, magnetite, monazite, and black tourmaline (schorl). However, when walking along the area where I thought the outcrop would be, I came across an outcrop of light green-layered rock. There were no indications of muscovite, magnetite, monazite, or tourmaline in the rock, and this was the only rock outcrop in the area. A closer look revealed that rocks resembled large pieces of green wood. They were like asbestos, but did not have a fibrous character. The rocks broke into large elongated fragments. Some of the pieces were 4 feet long and only 3 to 4 inches wide. They could be swung like a baseball bat.

I had a great deal of trouble describing the rocks. They were clearly not asbestos, and it was difficult to determine the mineral composition. Later review through the USGS (2005) indicated that the rock was actinolite schist of the Alligator Back Formation. This made sense, as the minerals were

The schist resembles asbestos but fortunately it does not have the fibers when inspected up close.

elongated and light green, and the rock appeared to be a metamorphic rock. Unfortunately, most of the site is on posted ground but some pieces can still be found in the road right–of–way.

References: Penick, 1987; USGS, 2016

20. Fairy Stone State Park
Sericite–Staurolite Crosses

The best way to find the fairy stones is to have a seat and look for the crosses on the ground.

See map page 100.
County: Patrick
Site type: Loose rocks along trails
Land status: State Park, but collecting of Fairy Stones allowed
Material: "Fairy Stone," which are sericite after staurolite penetration twins
Host rock: Late Precambrian-Early Cambrian Fork Mountain Formation Schist and Gneiss
Difficulty: Easy
Family-friendly: Yes
Tools needed: None, no digging allowed, only picking crystals from surface
Special concerns: Mosquitoes and mud. Lot of sitting on bare ground, can get messy after rain
Special attractions: Fairy Stone State Park
GPS parking: N36°45′29″ / W80°05′28″

The staurolite has been almost entirely replaced by sericite but the stones have kept their original shapes.

Topographic quadrangle: Philpott Lake, VA

Finding the site: From the gate at Fairy Stone State Park, proceed south on VA-346 and turn left (east) onto VA-57. Proceed 3.8 miles to a gasoline station on the left (north) side of the road and park here. You will see some picnic tables on the west side of the gas station. This is State Park Property. From here, hike onto the trail. The staurolite crystals are found on the ground throughout the area. You do not need to pay to park here, but I still recommend entering the park and visiting the visitor center to get oriented and get some tips on finding fairy stones.

Rockhounding

This is a great site for anyone that enjoys walking and looking for crystals on the ground. The "fairy stones" are penetration twins that were originally staurolite, but they have been almost entirely replaced by sericite and chlorite. The penetration twins form crosses, and they formed as porphyroblasts in schists and gneiss. The crosses later weathered out of the rocks. They are found on the surface where the staurolite-bearing rocks crop out on the surface.

My experience with staurolite crosses is that they can be notoriously difficult to find unless you are in the right spot. We first stopped at the State Park

This is a typical crystal that is found on the ground. The well-defined sides make it easy to spot.

to get oriented, and the park ranger in the gift shop was extremely helpful. He said that the only place in the park with the fairy stones is the section of the park just west of the gas station. This was important, as without this information I might have started looking elsewhere in the park and soon become discouraged.

He gave us clear directions and some key tips. No digging tools are allowed, but you do not need to dig any holes. The most important tip was to look at the ground and watch for "diamonds" and "boxes." These shapes are indicative of the fairy stones, and when you see a straight line, angle, or corner on the ground, it is often a sericite after staurolite penetration twin. This is a mouthful, so perhaps it is best to stick with the nontechnical name "fairy stone."

We found about thirty to forty fairy stones between three people in about one hour. The hiking trails were fairly flat and it was easy walking. The site is popular as several families and couples visited, and everyone found fairy stones. This is a well-managed park, and I really appreciate the Virginia Department of Conservation and Recreation for keeping this area open for mineral collecting.

References: Henika, 1971; Moore, 1937; Penick, 1987; USGS, 2005

BLUE RIDGE

21. Happy Creek Epidotized Granite and Metabasalt

The rocks are located west of the road along Happy Creek.

County/City: Warren County
Site type: Streamside rocks
Land status: Private and National Park Service
Material: Epidotized granite and metabasalt
Host rock: Precambrian Metabasalt of the Catoctin Formation
Difficulty: Easy
Family-friendly: No, slopes on creek are steep
Tools needed: Hammer
Special concerns: Slopes on creek can be steep, collecting not allowed in the National Park
Special attractions: Shenandoah National Park
GPS parking: N38°53'06" / W78°10'20"
Topographic quadrangle: Front Royal, VA

Finding the site: From Front Royal, at the intersection of VA-55 and US 522, head south for 1.8 miles. Turn right (south) onto Harmony Hollow Road. Proceed 0.3 mile to the parking area, which will be on the left (east) side of the road. You will have to pass this and make a U-turn to best access the parking area. From here, walk a few hundred feet to the east bank of Happy Creek where many boulders and large rocks are present.

Rockhounding

Many of the streams along the flanks of Shenandoah National Park have an abundance of metabasalt and granite. Happy Creek along Harmony Hollow Road is no exception. The trickiest part of the site is to find safe parking. The boundaries of the National Park are marked along the creek, so you have a generally good idea where the Park Service property starts and ends.

We were able to find many pieces of purplish metabasalt, and many of these had bands of epidote. Some of the metabasalts have amygdules that were filled with a white mineral and epidote. Several other metabasalt pieces where dark gray–green and had a splatter of red. I assumed this was similar to the

This metabasalt has abundant green epidote.

Bands of apple green epidote are common at this site.

"bloodstone" that had been referenced by Eckert (2000) as occurring in Page County by Luray. Some granite boulders in the creek had abundant epidote and could be considered to be unakite, but it was more difficult to find the granitic pieces than the metabasalt. I did not find many granites that also had abundant orange feldspar so I was reluctant to consider this a good unakite locality.

References: Eckert, 2000; Rader and Biggs, 1975

Sites 21–23

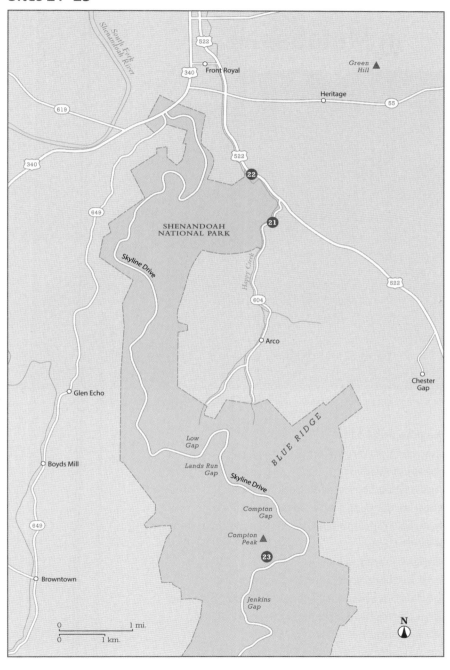

22. Front Royal Chrysotile in Metabasalt

The metabasalts are adjacent to the road and thick with poison ivy in the summer.

See map page 111.
County/City: Warren County
Site type: Roadcut
Land status: Shenandoah National Park
Material: Bands of white chrysotile asbestos
Host rock: Precambrian Catoctin Formation metabasalt
Difficulty: Easy
Family-friendly: Yes
Tools needed: None, no collecting allowed
Special concerns: Heavy vegetation and poison ivy
Special attractions: Shenandoah National Park
GPS parking: N38°53'40" / W78°10'43"
Topographic quadrangle: Front Royal, VA

White chrysolite is easy to see in the outcrops.

Finding the site: From Front Royal, at the intersection of VA-55 and US-522, head south for 1.2 miles. Park in the wide area along the shoulder. Plenty of parking is available. From here, walk southeast on US-522 for about 200 feet. The chrysotile bands are in the metabasalt exposed on the south side of the road. Some bands are also present in areas along the north side of the road.

Rockhounding

This is both an easy locality to find and an easy one to miss if you are not looking for it. I had heard of chrysotile asbestos in the region, and while driving along Rte. 522 my wife noticed large white bands in the metabasalt outcrops on the south side of the road. White bands in metabasalt likely meant chrysotile. These were underneath overhangs in the exposures and the area was also covered by vegetation. We were able to find a place to park and get out to look at the exposures more closely.

The bands are 2 to 3 inches wide and are fibrous. They are off-white to light green and stand out against the metabasalt. Many of the fibrous areas are confined to the rock surface, and they appear to have formed along shear

This white chrysotile was seen on the north side of the road and it easy to see against the rocks.

zones in the rocks. We later found some additional bands on the north side of US-522. I suspect that if you look closer you will be able to find many more zones. It would be especially interesting to visit in the winter when the vegetation is gone as long as the outcrops are not covered by snow. Since these metabasalts with chrysotile are within the National Park, collecting is not allowed, but the chrysotile bands are so large that they are still worth seeing.

Reference: Rader and Biggs, 1975

23. Compton Peak Columnar Metabasalt

The columnar basalt is one of the most spectacular rock outcrops in the eastern United States.

See map page 111.
County/City: Rappahannock County
Site type: Outcrop
Land status: Shenandoah National Park

The columnar jointing formed from the 120 degree angles of stress-relief fractures as the basalt cooled.

Material: Columnar metabasalt
Host rock: Precambrian Catoctin Formation metabasalt
Difficulty: Easy
Family-friendly: Yes
Tools needed: None
Special concerns: No collecting allowed in the National Park, fee to enter the park
Special attractions: Shenandoah National Park
GPS parking: N38°49'25" / W78°10'14"
GPS columnar basalt: N38°48'58" / W78°10'29"
Topographic quadrangle: Chester Gap, VA
Finding the site: From Front Royal, take US 340 South, and turn right (south) onto Skyline Drive. Continue approximately 10.4 miles to the trailhead parking area, which will be on the left (east) side of Skyline Drive. Park here and hike southward on the Appalachian Trail for approximately 1.2 miles. Follow a short trail from the main trail to the basalt columns. The area is well marked and is easy to find as it is a major feature to see from this part of the Appalachian Trail.

Rockhounding

While rock collecting is not allowed in Shenandoah National Park, there are many geologic features that rockhounds will find worth visiting. The basalt columns exposed at this locality are striking, and they are positioned at an angle which shows the hexagonal cooling pattern in the basalt.

You must watch your step as you approach the columns as the area is rocky and uneven.

The basalts were flood basalts that erupted and covered a wide area. They were not immediately cooled by ocean water, which would have resulted in pillow basalts. They were not infused with gases, which would have resulted in vesicles and other features caused by gas bubbles. I have found some vesicular basalt on nearby trails, but these columnar basalts are solid and nearly free of vesicles. The basalts got to cool slowly, but as they were cooling, they formed a hexagonal pattern.

Hexagons are common in nature as a result of stress relief. As the lava cooled and shrank, tensional stresses developed in the rock. A hexagonal system provides the greatest stress relief with the fewest cracks. Angles of 120 degrees provide the greatest relief, and when these are joined, a hexagonal pattern develops. Perfect hexagons are rare as cooling stresses are never constant. The resulting pattern is generally close enough to provide the appearance of hexagons.

This is one of the most spectacular outcrops in the eastern United States. It is fortunate that it is within the National Park. The outcrop and access are protected and it will be preserved for many future generations.

References: Huber and Eckhardt, 1999; USGS, 2005

24. Rose River Granite and Unakite

The bed of the Rose River is full of rocks from the core of the Blue Ridge Mountains.

County/City: Madison County
Site type: Stream bed
Land status: Private but not posted, along road
Material: Colorful granite and unakite
Host rock: Precambrian granitic and metamorphic rocks
Difficulty: Hard
Family-friendly: Yes
Tools needed: Hammer, but best rocks are loose in stream bed
Special concerns: Remote area, must approach from southeast
Special attractions: Shenandoah National Park
GPS parking: N38°30'37.8" / W78°21'23.7"
GPS stream bed: N38°30'37" / W78°21'23"
Topographic quadrangle: Old Rag Mountain, VA

This granite has blue quartz, and blue quartz is common in the granitic rocks in the Rose River.

Finding the site: From US-29 south of Culpeper, take VA-609 west for 7.5 miles. Turn right (west) onto VA-231 and continue for 0.6 mile. Take a slight left (west) onto VA-670, and proceed to the site. Cross the Rose River, turnaround, and park on the south side of the road just west of the bridge. Unakite and granite can be found on both the downstream and upstream sides of the bridge.

Rockhounding

This is a well-known locality for unakite. Unfortunately it appears to be too well known as it also appears to be picked over. While I found it difficult to find the unakite, I found an abundance of granite with orange feldspar and blue quartz, and lots of colorful metabasalt, but did not find any pieces that I would consider to be excellent examples of unakite.

The area is outside of Shenandoah National Park. It appears to be private land but is not posted. There are also signs that the Rose River is a stocked trout water. This is excellent as it means that fisherman access this area. I did

Although the streambed has millions of rocks, it takes a sharp eye to find the unakite.

not have to worry so much about getting kicked out. I did not get to stay as long as I would have liked, and I am confident that I would have found better unakite with a little more time and effort. Despite the difficulties in finding unakite at this site, it is still among the most scenic rock collecting sites in the Blue Ridge, and I highly recommend the visit.

Reference: Eckert, 2000

Sites 24–25

25. Stanley Unakite

The access point to Hawksbill Creek is on the east side of VA-624 just south of the bridge over the creek.

See map page 121.
County/City: Page County
Site type: Stream bed
Land status: Private but not posted, along road
Material: Unakite and other colorful rocks
Host rock: Precambrian granitic and metamorphic rocks
Difficulty: Easy
Family-friendly: No, as this required wading in stream with steep slope
Tools needed: Hammer, but best rocks are loose in stream bed
Special concerns: Must be careful of road traffic
Special attractions: Shenandoah National Park
GPS parking: N38°34'30" / W78°28'43"
GPS access to stream: N38°34'27" / W78°28'43"
Topographic quadrangle: Big Meadows, VA

Rounded granitic rocks are abundant in Hakwsbill Creek.

Finding the site: From Luray, at the intersection of Business US-211 and Business US-340, turn south on US-340. Continue 6.0 miles, and make a slight left (southeast) onto VA-624. Proceed 0.6 mile and turn left (east) onto VA-689. Continue about 500 feet to a parking area. This is operated by the Town of Stanley-Public Works. I recommend parking here and walking to the site. The access point to Hawksbill Creek is on the west side of the creek.

Rockhounding

Hawksbill Creek is well known as a creek that has unakite. The unakite is derived from the epidotized granite in the mountains east of Stanley and at the headwaters of the creek. Much of Hawksbill Creek goes through private land, and we were not able to find many sections that gave us access to the creek.

This locality has good parking and I was able to climb into the creek to look for rocks. The creek is relatively shallow during the summer. The west bank is covered with gray limestone, and many of these rocks are loose, so you

The bed of Hawksbill Creek is loaded with rocks and many of them contain epidote.

have to be careful when going to the creek. I quickly found many colorful igneous rocks including granite and metabasalt. However, I was disappointed that I did not find as much unakite as I had hoped for. I suspect that this area may have been picked over, but more unakite will wash down this creek with the next floods.

References: Eckert, 2000; Penick, 1987

26. Kennedy Mine Limonite and Manganese Oxides

The floor of the former mine is a wide flat area in the woods next to the road.

County/City: Augusta County
Site type: Former open pit mine
Land status: George Washington National Forest
Material: Limonite and manganese oxides
Host rock: Cambrian Shady Dolomite
Difficulty: Medium
Family-friendly: Yes
Tools needed: Hammer and gloves
Special concerns: Lot of leaf cover and vegetation
Special attractions: Shenandoah National Park
GPS parking: N37°58'17" / W79°00'10"
Topographic quadrangle: Big Levels, VA

Finding the site: From the intersection of US-340 and VA-608 in Stuarts Draft, take VA-608 south for 1.5 miles. This turns into VA-610. Continue southeast for 0.4 mile, and turn right (south) onto VA-660. Go 2.3 miles, and turn left (east) onto Coal Road. Continue 2.1 miles on Coal Road. The parking area is on the left. The mine is a large open depression south of Coal Road.

Rockhounding

The Kennedy Mine last operated from 1917 to 1918 when several carloads of ore that averaged more than 40 percent manganese were shipped. Today the mine is barely recognizable and is overgrown with trees and other vegetation. The mine area is a open pit that is surrounded by sloping highwalls that are about 15 feet high. Trees have grown on the floor and along the highwalls.

You cannot see this mine from the road, so it is extremely easy to miss while you are driving on Coal Road. You should use GPS coordinates to find the site, and I also recommend obtaining an older copy of the Big Levels, VA, topographic map if available. The mine is marked on this map. Unfortunately, the latest USGS topographic maps eliminate all modern and historic cultural features, so the mine is not marked on recent maps. I also recommend boots and gloves as the brush cover is thick in places and some of the lower areas are water saturated.

This small nodule had an interior of powdered limonite.

The hematite and manganese oxide nodules are often found on loose on the ground where soils are exposed.

I walked throughout the open pit and looked for manganese minerals and also kept an eye open for other minerals. It was difficult to find manganese minerals and you have to make some effort at this site. I found some small pieces of manganese oxides and limonite on top of what I interpreted as the northern edge of the mine just south of the road. The manganese minerals are easy to spot as they are generally black with some limonite, and they are much denser than the surrounding rocks. I also found a small piece of limonite that was much less dense than expected. Cracking this open revealed a hollow interior.

If you come to this site, try to allow for adequate time to look for the minerals. There likely is a dump area that has stockpiled ore but it is almost certainly covered by trees and vegetation. I also recommend looking online for the references that describe this mine, such as Knechtel (1943) and Werner (1966) and using their maps as a guide as well. Werner shows this mine as at the site that I visited, but maps from Knechtel, which are more detailed, indicate that the actual mine workings may be further south. Looking at historic air photos on Google Earth may also be useful.

References: Knechtel, 1943; Werner, 1966; USGS, 2005

Sites 26–27

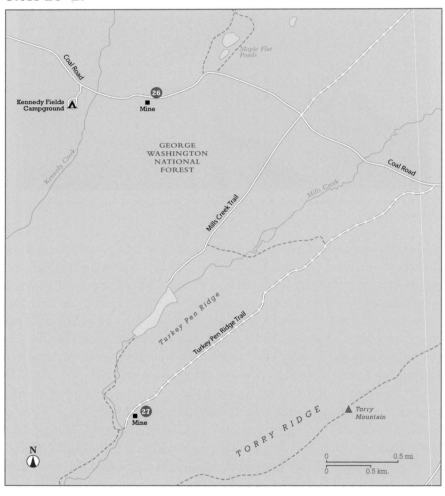

Coal Road

Maple Flat Ponds

Kennedy Fields Campground

26

Mine

Kennedy Creek

GEORGE WASHINGTON NATIONAL FOREST

Coal Road

Mills Creek

Mills Creek Trail

Turkey Pen Ridge

Turkey Pen Ridge Trail

27

Mine

Torry Mountain

TORRY RIDGE

N

0   0.5 mi.
0   0.5 km.

27. Mount Torry Mine Limonite and Hematite

The former mine area is covered by woods and is hard to identify from the trail.

See map page 128.
County/City: Augusta County
Site type: Former open pit mine
Land status: George Washington National Forest
Material: Limonite and hematite
Host rock: Cambrian Antietam Formation Sandstone and Shady Dolomite
Difficulty: Hard
Family-friendly: Yes, but a long hike to the mine site
Tools needed: Hammer and gloves
Special concerns: Long hike, must allow adequate time at site
Special attractions: Shenandoah National Park
GPS parking: N37°57'48" / W78°58'16"
GPS mine site: N37°56'34" / W79°00'16"

Some of the sandstones are rich in hematite.

Topographic quadrangle: Big Levels, VA
Finding the site: From I-64, take exit 96 to VA-624 south. This becomes South Delphine Avenue and soon turns into Mount Torrey Road. At the intersection of VA-624 and VA-664 in Lyndhurst, turn left (south) to continue on Mount Torrey Road, which is now VA-664. Continue 4.8 miles, and turn right (west) onto Coal Road. Proceed 0.5 mile to the trailhead, which is on the left (south) side of coal road. It is a well-marked trail head with parking for a few cars. From the trailhead, hike 2.4 miles on the Turkey Pen Ridge Trail to the Mount Torry Mine site.

Rockhounding

The Mount Torry Mine was one of the main producers of manganese in this region. The mine was reportedly last mined in the early twentieth century. Today it is heavily overgrown, and it is difficult to tell that it was a mine.

You should allow adequate time to visit this site, and I recommend visiting early in the day. The hike to the mine site is generally level and pleasant, but it is 2.4 miles from the trailhead. I visited the site very late in the afternoon and got caught in the woods after dark, which was not a pleasant experience.

This sandstone was red on the outside and has pink banks exposed in its interior.

The mine site has some small ridges that appear to be mine tailings. South of the trail is a broad area that appears to have been cleared in the past, and I checked some of the small drainages for indications of manganese minerals. I did not find any manganese, but I found some limonite and pieces of sandstone that were rich in hematite and limonite and were a bright orange red when broken apart. This iron-stained sandstone is likely from the Antietam Formation Sandstone. The mine is near the contact with the Antietam Formation and the underlying Shady Dolomite. The area is mapped as Antietam Sandstone, but Werner (1966) states that the mine workings were in the Shady Dolomite.

This is another site where I recommend looking online for the references that describe this mine, such as Knechtel (1943) and Werner (1966) and using their maps as a guide. Werner shows this area as the Mount Torry Mine. I suspect I may have just missed some of the key workings, but the trees and brush make them easy to miss. Looking at historic air photos on Google Earth may also be useful.

References: Knechtel, 1943; Werner, 1966; USGS, 2005

28. Pkin Limonite

Some of the rocks have concentric bands of yellow and brown limonite.

County/City: Augusta County
Site type: Former open pit mine
Land status: George Washington National Forest
Material: Limonite
Host rock: Cambrian Shady Dolomite
Difficulty: Medium
Family-friendly: Yes, but a long hike to the mine site
Tools needed: Hammer and gloves
Special concerns: Long hike, must allow adequate time at site
Special attractions: Shenandoah National Park
GPS parking: N37°55′30″ / W79°09′04″
GPS mine site: N37°55′08″ / W79°09′48″
Topographic quadrangle: Vesuvius, VA
Finding the site: From I-81, take exit 205 for VA-606 to Steeles Tavern. Continue 1.5 miles on VA-606, and then turn left (northeast) on US-11N. Go 0.1 mile, and

turn right (southeast) onto VA-56E. Go 1.1 miles, and then turn left (northeast) onto SR 608. Proceed 1.1 miles, and park at the end of the road. Follow the trail in the woods 0.8 mile to the limonite mines.

Rockhounding

According to Werner (1966), this site was the Black Rock Mine, which produced iron oxide. This is one of the best limonite collecting sites that I have seen in the Blue Ridge Province. We were very fortunate to find this site as we were originally trying to the reach the mines from VA-608. All the properties along the road were private and this kept us from reaching the mines. Fortunately, when looking at rocks along the railroad tracks, we spoke with a local. He suggested taking Spy Hook Road and parking at the end of the road. The trail at this site would then lead to the iron mines. He made the comment, "Ain't no one gonna bother you back there!"

We parked at the trailhead and hiked to the mines. The trail is indistinct, but it was clearly shown on Google Maps on my phone. We hiked to the end of the trail, and we began to find limonite on the trail and on the sides.

The former mined areas have left rounded cuts in the hillside.

Circular depressions are often former mining pits and sometimes limonite can be found in and near these pits.

We looked for large, dense orange rocks, and broke them open. Many of these had black and brown bands. At the mine site area we found a large cut that appeared to be manmade on the northwest side of the trail. This area was heavily overgrown, but it was possible to climb down into the cut, and look for large pieces of limonite under the leaves and brush. Many of these pieces were dense and rich in iron oxides. Most of the oxides were limonite but there was some minor hematite. We also noticed many large circular depressions that were former prospecting pits. If you were not specifically looking for iron mines, you may not notice the features indicative of the mines. Information from Werner (1996) suggests that this iron mine may not have been worked since the end of the 1800s.

Reference: Werner, 1966

Sites 28–30

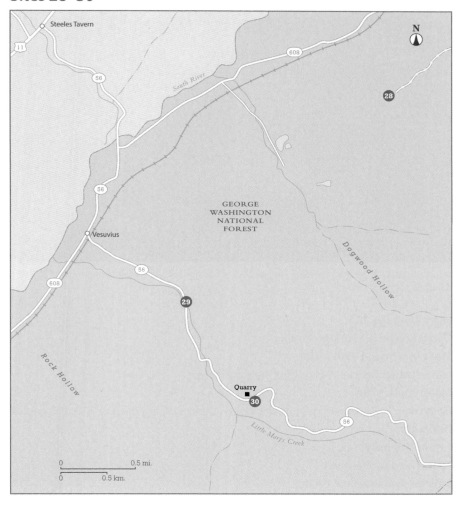

29. Little Marys Creek Unakite

This is a typical granite from the creek. The amounts of orange feldspar and light green epidote vary in the rocks.

See map page 135.
County/City: Rockbridge County
Site type: Stream bed rocks
Land status: George Washington National Forest
Material: Unakite
Host rock: Precambrian granitic and gneissic rocks of Virginia Blue Ridge Complex
Difficulty: Easy
Family-friendly: Yes
Tools needed: Hammer
Special concerns: Uncertain
Special attractions: Shenandoah National Park
GPS parking: N37°54'00" / W79°11'11"
Topographic quadrangle: Vesuvius, VA

Access to Little Marys Creek is best from the parking areas next to the bridges on VA-56.

Finding the site: From Vesuvius, take VA-56 east for approximately 0.8 mile. Stop at the turnout just west of the first bridge, which is on the south side of the road. Rocks are in Little Marys Creek. There is also unakite in Little Marys Creek near the next bridge east on VA-56, so this is really a site with two stops.

Rockhounding

I think this is one of the best places in Virginia to find unakite in a stream. The parking areas for both sites are very wide, and there are no signs prohibiting access into Little Marys Creek. Little Marys Creek is also quite little, and during the dry months it is very easy to step across.

The best way to find the unakite is to look for granitic rocks in the stream that are light green and orange. I also found that the banks just outside the stream have unakite. Most of the rocks in the stream and along the banks are gray or light brown, and you have to look for the light green and orange that stands out against this background. Many of the rocks that I found were almost entirely light green epidote, and it was challenging to find the best pieces that have both the orange feldspar and light green epidote.

Little Marys Creek is small but it is one of the best streams for finding unakite in the area.

Many of the best pieces of unakite are rounded, which suggests that they have been transported from further away and have been subject to more rounding and polishing by natural erosion than the flat and angular rocks. Unakite is also extremely hard. Many large pieces that I tried to break into manageable sizes could not be easily broken. I brought a foot-wide boulder out of the stream and tried to break it with a three-pound crack hammer, but finally gave up as it was too hard. Like many unakite sites in Virginia, I suspect this site has been picked over, but it was relatively easy to find unakite when compared with other unakite creek localities in Virginia.

Reference: Werner, 1966

30. Vesuvius Unakite Quarry

This quarry on VA-56 has bright orange feldspar in many of the rocks.

See map page 135.
County: Rockbridge County
Site type: Former quarry
Land status: Likely George Washington National Forest, but may have private sections
Material: Unakite
Host rock: Precambrian granitic and gneissic rocks of Virginia Blue Ridge Complex
Difficulty: Easy
Family-friendly: Yes
Tools needed: Hammer
Special concerns: Very brushy area, land status ambiguous
Special attractions: Shenandoah National Park
GPS parking: N37°53'28" / W79°10'45"
Topographic quadrangle: Vesuvius, VA

The parking area is marked with large rocks and is large enough for one or two cars at the most.

Finding the site: From Vesuvius, take VA-56 east for approximately 1.6 miles. The unakite quarry is on the north side of VA-56 just before a sharp bend in the road. The parking area is easy to spot as there are large boulders set off on the road shoulder, and this makes a small area for parking. Parking is limited to two cars at the most.

Rockhounding

This is a well-known locality for unakite. I have spoken to many people who have collected at the site. The area is mapped as within George Washington National Forest, and it is clearly marked on topographic maps and referenced in the geological literature. I did not see any no-trespassing signs, but some people have told me that it is owned by the farm just across the road. However, I have not spoken to this landowner.

We first visited this site on a late afternoon after a rainstorm. We hiked into the woods and found several boulders with weathered white and orange feldspar. The orange feldspar was prominent and many of the pieces did not

The former quarry is well exposed near VA-56 but the rocks exposed in this area are highly weathered.

have the green epidote. The area was extremely brushy and difficult for hiking. We found many weathered pieces with orange feldspar.

As we were getting ready to leave we found that the main part of the quarry highwall was not in the woods north of the parking area, but just east of the parking area. This is a large cliff of weathered granitic rock. Some of the rocks of this area had the green epidote with the orange feldspar, but many of the rocks were extremely weathered.

It takes some effort to find unweathered unakite at this locality, but it should be possible to find if you look. The site has the big advantage that you do not have to go for an extended hike. I highly recommend long pants and gloves if you intend to bushwack into the sections of the quarry that are covered in brush and not as well picked-over as the sites next to the parking area and highwall.

References: Penick, 1987; Werner, 1966; Wilkes et al., 2007

31. Tye River Blue Quartz

The best blue quartz is found in quartz-rich gneissic rocks in the river bed.

County/City: Nelson County

Site type: Loose rocks and outcrops in the river bed

Land status: Private but not posted, along road

Material: Blue quartz

Host rock: Precambrian granitic and gneissic rocks of Virginia Blue Ridge Complex

Difficulty: Easy

Family-friendly: Yes

Tools needed: Hammer

Special concerns: Access to Tye River is difficult as the sides are thick with brush

Special attractions: Shenandoah National Park

GPS parking: N37°45'19" / W78°59'16"

Topographic quadrangle: Horseshoe Mountain, VA

Finding the site: Parking is approximately 0.1 mile north of the intersection of VA-56 and VA-151. It is on the southwest bank of the Tye River. There is also a park-and-ride lot just east and north of the Tye River bridge on VA-151, and you can also walk to the locality from here.

Rockhounding

Robertson (1885) described a peculiar blue quartz from Nelson County, Virginia. This new variety of quartz, as described by Robertson, presented a characteristic waxy luster and a color varying from pale to deep blue. Wise (1981) said that the blue has been attributed to three basic causes: the partial reflection of light from inclusions, the scattering of light by closely spaced microfractures in the quartz, and the occurrence of scattered titanium as a coloring agent. Each of these can produce blue in quartz.

In Virginia, most blue quartz is found in the Blue Ridge Complex of granitic and gneissic rocks lying east of the Blue Ridge Mountains. The Blue Ridge Complex extends from Loudoun County in the north to Grayson County in the south. Some blue quartz is also reported in the Piedmont Province.

Wise described several localities for blue quartz in Virginia. The Tye River locality is relatively easy to access and has an abundance of river rocks with blue quartz. I visited the area in September 2016. The only problem with this site is that it can be extremely hard to reach the river through the briars and brush on the stream banks. I finally found an area near the river

Breaking apart this quartz-rich gneiss revealed an interior of waxy light blue quartz.

The Tye River, as seen from the VA-151 Bridge, is a broad shallow stream and is best accessed during low water.

that provided access, and from there I walked along the stream looking for blue quartz.

This is a locality where you need a hammer to crack open the rocks. Many of the rocks are covered with algae and sediment, and most of them appear dark brown to black. Breaking open some of the gneissic rocks reveals that many of them have light blue quartz crystals. The best rocks are the ones that show a hint of white through the algae and sediment. Break these open, and you may be rewarded with a section of blue quartz. If you are not concerned with getting wet, you may want to cross to the opposite bank and try to find outcrops of gneissic bedrock with blue quartz. At the time of my visit, the river was relatively shallow, but I am sure that during the floods this is a full river. If possible you should time your collecting visits for periods of low water levels.

References: Robertson, 1885; Wise, 1981

Sites 31–32

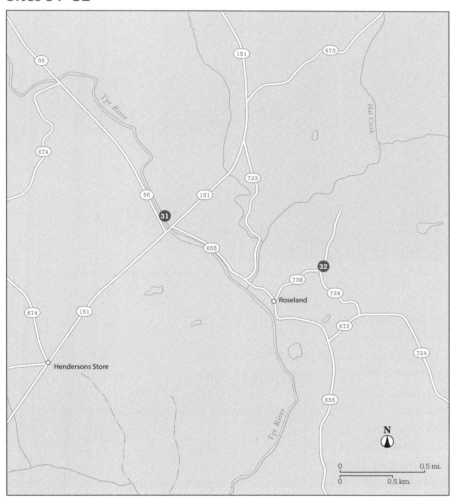

32. Roseland Blue Quartz

Pieces of weathered white gneiss with blue quartz can be found next to the woods on Gunter Hollow Road.

See map page 145.

County: Nelson County

Site type: Roadcut and loose rocks on roadside

Land status: Private but not posted, along road

Material: Blue quartz

Host rock: Precambrian granitic and gneissic rocks of Virginia Blue Ridge Complex

Difficulty: Easy

Family-friendly: Yes

Tools needed: Hammer

Special concerns: Roadcut is covered by vegetation and leaves, hard to see rocks

Special attractions: Shenandoah National Park

GPS parking: N37°45'02" / W78°58'16"

Topographic quadrangle: Horseshoe Mountain, VA

The blue quartz often appears as gray streaks within the rocks.

Finding the site: Start at the intersection of VA-56 and VA-151. Head north on VA-151 and immediately after crossing the Tye River bridge, turn right (southeast) on VA-655, and continue for 0.7 mile. Turn left on VA-738 (Gunter Hollow Road), and continue for 0.4 mile to the intersection with VA-724 (Mt. Rouge Road). The blue quartz can be found along the roadside and in loose rocks on the slope east side of Mt. Rouge Road.

Rockhounding

This is an unusual locality as nearly all the blue quartz is found as loose rocks and not in outcrop. I parked at this site after a series of rainstorms, and as soon as I got out of my car I noticed white rocks with beautiful blue quartz. Many of these rocks had washed onto the road. The blue quartz is light blue to gray and waxy in appearance.

I walked along the side of Mt. Rouge Road, but could not find any actual outcrops. However, I did find several large white rocks. When cracked open, many of them had sections of light blue quartz.

I later found that I went to a different locality than I intended. I had been led to the site by an independent website that marked the roadcut on a map, and only VA-724 was labeled, and I mistakenly went to the wrong road intersection. However, I was still able to find blue quartz at this site. I later reviewed the locality information in Wise (1981) for Nelson County blue quartz localities, and his suggested location is a roadcut near the intersection of 724 and 655. Using Google Maps Street View, I checked the nearby areas and found a prominent outcrop of gray rocks at 37°44'51"N / 78°58'32"W on the north side of VA-655, which is 0.4 mile west of the intersection of VA-655 and VA-724. This may have been the outcrop that I had originally intended to visit. This is a location I will be sure to check the next time I am near Roseland.

Reference: Wise, 1981

VALLEY AND RIDGE

33. Gainesboro Fossils

Many of the fossils are small but abundant in some of the rocks.

County: Frederick
Site type: Roadcuts
Land status: Uncertain, but none of the land is posted
Material: Fossils
Host rock: Middle Devonian Mahantango Formation
Difficulty: Moderate
Family-friendly: No, due to heavy traffic on US Rte. 522
Tools needed: Hammer
Special concerns: Very brushy, ticks, some climbing on loose rocks on steep slope
Special attractions: None
GPS parking: N39°18′13″ / W78°16′56″
Topographic quadrangle: Gore, VA-WV
Finding the site: Take US 522 north to where it is crossed by VA-705, which is also known as Ebenezer Church Road. Continue approximately 0.5 mile north, and turn around so you are now heading southeast. Park in the broad shoulder on the

The best collecting is in loose rocks on this hillside just north of the parking area.

southwest side of US 522 just south of Fout Lane. Make certain that you park well away from the traffic. From here, walk up to the small ridge between the north and southbound lanes of US 522.

Rockhounding

This is Locality 28 in Burns (1991). The best fossil collecting at this site is near the top of the small ridge between US Rte. 522. This highway is very busy and wide, and you must be extremely careful when crossing. The best fossils are found in the loose rocks. All the fossils that I found were brachiopods and other small bivalves. The fossils occur as casts, and many of the brachiopods were almost an inch wide. Most of the fossils I found were on the hillside just north of the parking area. The best way to find the fossils is to look for loose rocks with layers of shells and break these apart.

Burns (1991) reported that quartz crystals could be found in the northernmost exposure on this ridge, but cautioned that the cliff is very close to the road. I attempted to walk toward this section but the traffic was heavy. It was too dangerous to get to this section. I did not get to this area and it was much safer to stay within the sections of ridge that were not exposed to traffic.

Looking through loose rocks in fossiliferous zones will guarantee fossils at this site.

The northbound lane has a long well-exposed section of rocks, and I checked this area for fossils. The sections that I checked were barren and I did not find any notable fossils. If you go to this site I recommend focusing on the ridge between the two highways. The land in this section was not posted against trespassing. Since it is in Burn's book it has undoubtedly seen many fossil hunters, but many fossils remain for collectors.

Reference: Burns, 1991

Sites 33–34

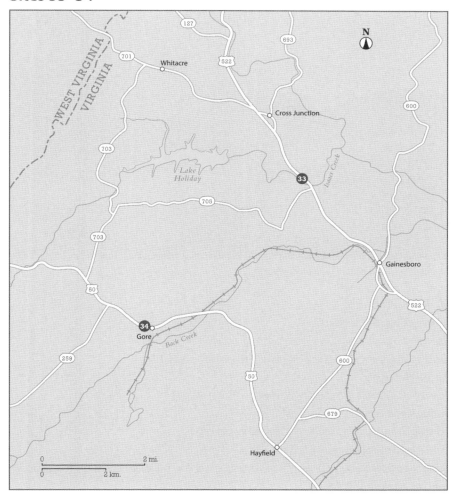

34. Gore Fossils

The outcrop is just north of Gore on the highway.

See map page 153.
County/City: Frederick
Site type: Roadcuts
Land status: Uncertain, but none of the land is posted.
Material: Fossils
Host rock: Middle Devonian Mahantango Formation
Difficulty: Moderate
Family-friendly: No, due to heavy traffic on US-50
Tools needed: Hammer
Special concerns: Very brushy, ticks, some climbing on loose rocks on steep slope
Special attractions: None
GPS parking: N39°15′54″ / W78°20′04″
GPS outcrops: N39°15′53″ / W78°19′57″
Topographic quadrangle: Gore, VA-WV

Splitting open the shale can reveal fossils.

Finding the site: From VA-37, take the US-50 exit toward Winchester/Romney. After you turn west onto US-50, proceed 10.4 miles west. The site is just north of the small town of Gore. A small parking area is present just east of the Volunteer Fire and Rescue Company 14, which is just west of the fossil-bearing outcrops. Park here and walk to the outcrops.

Rockhounding

This is Site 22 in Burns (1991). This is a long road cut on the north side of Hwy. 50 just north of Gore, Virginia. The shoulder is too small for parking safely. At the far west end of the roadcut, there is a small private road next to the Gore Volunteer Fire and Rescue Company. We parked here, and I walked to the roadcut. Fortunately you do not have to cross the road. The best fossils are found in the loose rocks along the base of the roadcut. All the fossils that I found were brachiopods and other small bivalves. The fossils occur as casts and many of the brachiopods were almost an inch wide. The best way to find the fossils is to look for loose rocks with layers of shells and break these apart.

The outcrop is off the road but you must still wear a high-visibility safety vest and be very careful of traffic.

Burns (1991) reported that trilobites were abundant at this site, but I did not find any trilobites. He also indicated that some of the better collecting was near the top of the roadcut, but I focused on the loose rocks next to the road for safety.

When I reviewed this area in Google Maps, the street view camera appeared to show fossil collectors on the eastern end of the roadcut. I could see a vehicle parked on the road, two people with colored vests, and two white buckets. This suggests this is a popular fossil collecting site. It should remain a good locality as long as it does not become posted against trespassing.

Reference: Burns, 1991

35. Elizabeth Furnace Slag, Limonite, and Hematite

Hematite can be seen around the former loading area of the furnace.

County/City: Shenandoah County
Site type: Former iron furnace
Land status: United States Forest Service Recreation Area
Material: Slag, limonite, and hematite
Host rock: Devonian Ridgely Sandstone and Helderberg Limestones
Difficulty: Easy
Family-friendly: Yes
Tools needed: None
Special concerns: Furnace is a State Park, collecting not allowed
Special attractions: Shenandoah National Park
GPS parking: N38°55'39" / W78°19'46"
GPS furnace: N38°55'44" / W78°19'38"

Topographic quadrangle: Strasburg, VA
Finding the site: From Strasburg, from the intersection of US 11 and VA-55, take VA 55, which starts as East King Street, 5.1 miles to VA-678. Turn right (south) on VA-678, which is Fort Valley Road, and proceed 4.0 miles. Turn left, cross Passage Creek, and park at the parking area. Follow the trails south of Passage Creek to the Furnace. Stay on the trails that are just south of the creek. Other trails in the park lead to other areas and not the furnace.

Rockhounding

This is one of the most accessible and well–preserved furnaces that I have visited in Virginia. It has several explanatory signs along the trail and an excellent parking area. The trail to the furnace is a short loop that is a level hike.

Elizabeth Furnace was built in 1836. Pig iron from the furnace was used to make wrought iron. The plant almost certainly used slave labor for the worst parts of the furnace work. The furnace was reportedly an important supplier of iron to the confederate war effort. As such, it was a target, and it

Not much is left of the furnace and what remains is fenced.

This is a large slab of pig iron next to the remains of the furnace.

was reportedly burned by General David Hunter during the Civil War. The furnace was inactive from 1865 to 1883. The furnace was restarted in 1883, but it closed by 1889. It could not compete with the larger plants that were producing iron elsewhere in the United States.

One of the most interesting aspects of the preservation of this furnace is that some of the original ore piles remain around the loading area. The iron ore and limestone were dumped through the top of the furnace, and small mounds of limonite and hematite can be found on the hill just above the furnace. I found some bright red hematite and orange limonite in the woods just east of the furnace loading area, as well as some slag. This material cannot be collected but it is still interesting to observe.

References: National Park Service, 1999; Rader and Biggs, 1975

Sites 35–37

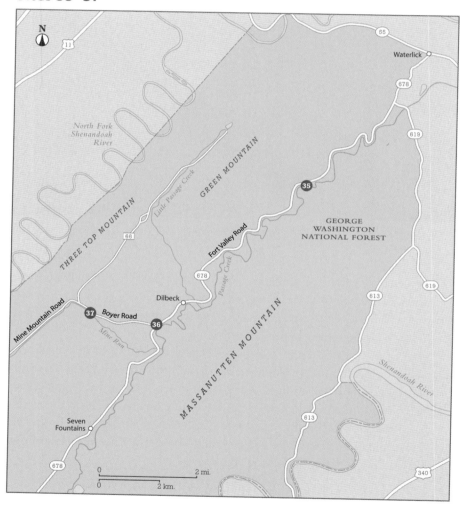

36. Fort Valley Road Fossils

Casts of brachiopods can be found at this site.

See map page 160.
County: Shenandoah
Site type: Roadcuts
Land status: Uncertain, but none of the land is posted
Material: Fossils
Host rock: Middle Devonian Mahantango Formation
Difficulty: Moderate
Family-friendly: Yes, traffic is very light
Tools needed: Hammer
Special concerns: Slopes are steep, collecting limited to loose rocks on roadcut
Special attractions: Elizabeth Furnace Recreation Area
GPS parking: N39°53'23" / W78°22'39"

The fossil-bearing outcrops are on the west side of Fort Valley Road.

Topographic quadrangle: Toms Brook, VA
Finding the site: From I-66, take exit 6 to US 522 South. Go about 1.2 miles, and turn right (west) onto VA 55 west. Proceed about 5.1 miles and turn left (south) on SR 678. Continue 8.6 miles to Boyer Road. Park on the south side of Boyer Road at this intersection. Parking is limited.

Rockhounding

This is Locality 30 in Burns (1991). This is a relatively short roadcut when compared with many of the other fossil–bearing roadcuts in northern Virginia. The area is remote and the traffic is light, but you still must be alert for traffic when collecting. The best fossils that I found were on the eastern side of the roadcut adjacent to Passage Creek. At first I did not find any fossils, but soon found some loose pieces with beds of fossils. The area initially appeared to be rather barren.

Another fossil collector arrived at the site during our visit. He had collected at this site numerous times and said that it was picked over. He then

Look for uneven patterns of fossil beds in the rocks, and crack the rocks open along these lines to expose fossils.

showed me numerous large intact sections of fossils at approximately eye level or higher. The fossil-bearing rocks can be distinguished by the presence of fossil beds. Cracking these open with a hammer always revealed abundant fossils.

Although the site may have been picked over, I still found many excellent fossils. This site should continue to produce fossils for the foreseeable future.

References: Burns, 1991; Rader and Biggs, 1975

37. Mine Gap Furnace Slag and Limonite

This glassy slag was found along the road next to the furnace.

See map page 160.
County: Shenandoah County
Site type: Former iron furnace
Land status: Furnace is private, but the ground next to the road is outside of posted ground
Material: Slag and limonite
Host rock: Silurian and Devonian Sediments, Helderberg and Cayugan Groups
Difficulty: Easy
Family-friendly: Yes
Tools needed: None
Special concerns: Furnace is private land, access is only to area adjacent to Boyer Road
Special attractions: Shenandoah National Park

The furnace is posted ground and just outside of the National Forest.

GPS parking: N38°53′34″ / W78°23′59″
Topographic quadrangle: Toms Brook, VA
Finding the site: From I-66, take exit 6 to US 522 South. Go about 1.2 miles, and turn right (west) onto VA 55 west. Proceed about 5.1 miles and turn left (south) on SR 678. Continue 8.6 miles and turn right (west) onto Boyer Road. Continue west for 1.3 miles. The furnace will be on your right. Parking is on the left (south) side of Boyer Road and just inside the National Forest Boundary.

Rockhounding

This is a former iron furnace that likely last operated in the mid– to late 1800s. The furnace is posted against trespassing, so without permission it is not possible to go onto the ground of the furnace. However, there is a strip along Boyer Road that is outside of the posted ground. I found several pieces of gray to green slag and pieces of limonite on the side of the road.

The furnace likely processed iron from the iron mines north of Mine Gap. Although the map shows this as National Forest, several landowners have

Parking for the site is just north of the sign for George Washington National Forest.

purchased the areas of the former mines. The former mine sites are heavily posted and should not be entered without permission.

Normally I would just drive by a site like this, but it is worth a stop to see the furnace and the area around it. As long as you stay out of the posted areas, you should be fine. The slag and limonite are not abundant, but the site is convenient as parking is right next to the site.

Reference: Rader and Biggs, 1975

38. Columbia Furnace Fossils

Crinoids are common in the rocks at this site.

County/City: Shenandoah County
Site type: Roadcut
Land status: George Washington National Forest
Material: Fossils
Host rock: Middle Devonian Mahantango Formation
Difficulty: Moderate
Family-friendly: Yes, traffic is very light
Tools needed: Hammer
Special concerns: Small area, slopes are steep
Special attractions: Wolf Gap Recreation Area
GPS parking: N38°53'45" / W78°40'02"
Topographic quadrangle: Wolf Gap, WV-VA

Parking is right next to the outcrop with the fossils.

Finding the site: From I-81, take either exit 283 to VA-42 or exit 279 to SR 675 to Columbia Furnace. From there, take SR 675 west for 2.9 miles to the intersection with SR 717. The parking area and roadcut are on the north side of SR 675. The roadcut is adjacent to the parking area and extends slightly to the east.

Rockhounding

This is Site 31 in Burns (1991). This is a great roadcut for fossil collecting as the parking is excellent and it is in a scenic area. It is a small roadcut and some of the best fossils are found by scrambling up the side of the cut. The Mahantango Formation is high in iron in this area and the rocks have some iron staining. The colors of the rocks include red, orange, and purple.

We found several brachiopods and crinoids. As in most parts of the Mahantango Formation, the best fossils tend to be along bedding planes where several fossils accumulated. The profiles of the fossil shells are exposed along these planes, and splitting the rocks along these planes generally reveals an abundance of fossils.

Site 38

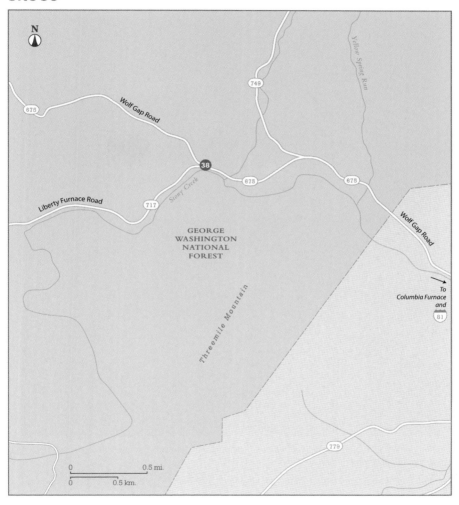

The outcrop is situated off the road side and fossils can be found in the loose rocks along the base of the outcrop.

Burns also noted that additional fossil–bearing roadcuts are present to the north along SR 675. Exploring these roadcuts may also reveal additional good areas for fossils.

Reference: Burns, 1991

39. Brocks Gap Limonite-Stained Rocks

The limonite occurs on the surfaces of broken rocks and forms yellow and brown patterns.

County: Rockingham County
Site type: Loose rocks at the base of large exposure
Land status: Highway right-of-way, land not posted
Material: Limonite-stained sediments
Host rock: Ordovician Shales and Mudstones and Silurian Sandstones
Difficulty: Easy
Family-friendly: Yes
Tools needed: Hammer
Special concerns: Parking is at an adjacent campground store, may want to ask permission to park
Special attractions: Shenandoah National Park
GPS parking: N38°38'32" / W78°51'42"
Topographic quadrangle: Timberville, VA

The outcrop is long and protected from traffic by a large guardrail.

Finding the site: From I-81, take exit 257 to VA-259 west. Continue 4.3 miles west, and turn left (west) onto East Lee Street. This turns into VA-259. Continue for 4.6 miles. Park at the parking area for the store/bar for the campground. The rocks are at the base of the large exposure of rocks on the east side of Brocks Gap.

Rockhounding

This is a site for decorative rocks. The shales, mudstones, and sandstones exposed at Brocks Gap are relatively uninteresting except for the limonite coatings on fractured surfaces. The base of the slope, which is steep, is covered with broken rocks. Some of these may be the crushed stone brought to the site during the construction of the road and guardrail.

The beds are nearly vertical and the rocks get younger as you walk to the west. Silurian and Devonian sandstones and limestones are present in the rocks to the west. A spectacular geologic feature is Chimney Rock, which is a vertical bed of Devonian Ridgely Sandstone. The area surrounding Chimney Rock appeared to be posted so I did not try to hike to this feature.

The guardrail is good protection from the traffic on VA-259. The best place to enter is by the east end of the guardrail. Go around the rail and walk

Limonitic rocks can be found in the broad ditch between the guardrail and the exposed hillside of Brocks Gap.

west along the drainage ditch. I visited the site in late summer when it was dry. During the spring and wet periods, this drainage may have standing water. The rocks are all loose and can be trimmed with a hammer to knock off the non-limonitic areas. Fossils are also reported in the Brocks Gaps sediments, but I did not see any fossils during my visit to this site.

References: Rader and Perry, 1976; USGS, 2005

Site 39–40

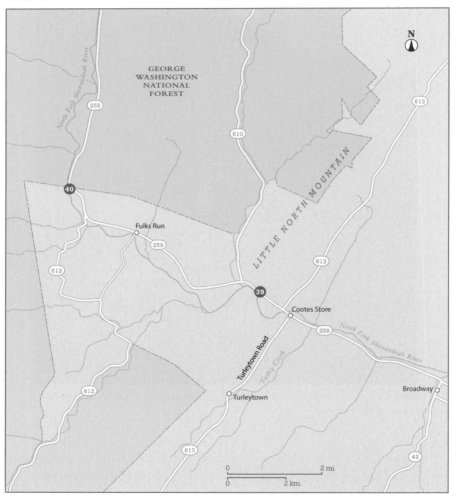

40. Fulks Run Fossils and Calcite

The fossils are within the limestone and are best exposed on weathered surfaces.

See map page 174.
County: Rockingham County
Site type: Roadcut
Land status: Highway right-of-way, land not posted
Material: Fossils and calcite crystals
Host rock: Silurian-Devonian Limestone of the Helderberg Group
Difficulty: Easy
Family-friendly: Yes
Tools needed: Hammer
Special concerns: Traffic on VA-259 is heavy
Special attractions: Shenandoah National Park
GPS parking: N38°40'21" / W78°55'41"

It is easy to park well off VA-259, but you have to cross this busy road to get to the outcrops.

Topographic quadrangle: Fulks Run, VA
Finding the site: From I-81, take exit 257 to VA-259 west. Continue 4.3 miles west, and turn left (west) onto East Lee Street. This turns into VA-259. Continue for 8.3 miles. Park at the large broad shoulder on the left (south) side of VA-259. The outcrop is directly across the highway.

Rockhounding

This is Site 13 in Burns (1991). This is a nice site as you can easily and safely park on the broad shoulder. The traffic on 259 is heavy but at least you should be able to park safely. I recommend wearing a bright yellow or orange safety vest, even though the outcrop is positioned safely off the road. The outcrop with fossils is weathered limestone of the Helderberg Group. Most of the fossils are relatively small and are crinoid columns and corals. The best pieces with fossils are on the weathered limestone surfaces. It is best to find hand samples of loose rock with the fossils exposed on the surface. Breaking the limestone open does not reveal the fossils as well as natural weathering.

The limestone outcrops are easy to see on the north side of VA-259.

Small calcite crystals can also be found in the outcrop, and many of these are in bedded gray calcareous shales. These can generally be broken out with a hammer. The calcite is not abundant, but it is still worth mentioning.

References: Burns, 1991; USGS, 2005

41. Maury River Pink and White Sandstone

Loose pink and white sandstone is near the spring with the sign warning against drinking the water.

County: Rockbridge County
Site type: Roadcuts
Land status: Uncertain. Area is used for tourism
Material: Pink and white sandstone
Host rock: Ordovician sandstone
Difficulty: Easy
Family-friendly: Yes
Tools needed: Hammer not recommended, collecting status uncertain
Special concerns: Traffic on VA-39 can be heavy
Special attractions: Maury River
GPS parking: N37°55'33" / W79°26'27"
Topographic quadrangle: Goshen, VA

Finding the site: From the intersection of VA-761 and VA-39, take VA-39 northwest along the west bank of the Maury River for 5.1 miles. Park on a turnoff on the east side of the road. Several loose white and pink rocks are just west of a sign that says "water not safe for drinking."

Rockhounding

The Maury River is a scenic river that flows southeastward through Rockbridge County. It was named for Commodore Matthew Fontaine Maury (1806–1873). Commodore Maury was an American naval officer and oceanographer. He wrote *The Physical Geography of the Sea* in 1855, which is considered to be the first textbook on modern oceanography. Although he was in the American Navy and was against slavery, he was from Virginia and took the side of the Confederacy during the Civil War. Rather than fight, he spent much of his time during the war overseas trying to encourage other nations to stop the war. A memorial to Maury is at Goshen Pass on the Maury River, and it is

This large boulder of pink and white sandstone was adjacent to the road.

The Maury River is in a scenic canyon and is a popular spot for both locals and Virginia tourists.

close to this sandstone locality. Commodore Maury was also a geologist, and I am sure he would have appreciated this locality along the Maury River.

I came to this site as Penick (1992) indicated that a pink limestone suitable for various cabochons and ornaments is along the Maury River near Rockbridge Baths on the south side of VA-39. I drove through Rockbridge

Site 41

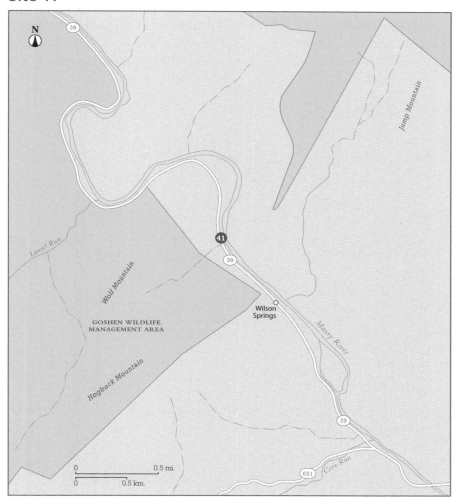

Baths but did not see any outcrops. However, outcrops are abundant in Goshen Pass. I drove up the Pass and looked at the outcrops. Most of them were white to gray to light pink. I found some nice pink rocks near a spring. They resembled a sandy limestone and I thought this might be the limestone referred to by Penick (1992). The sandstone was next to a sign stating that the water was not safe to drink. I also checked the larger outcrops to the west. These appeared to be white sandstone.

I later checked the rocks with hydrochloric acid to see if they would effervesce with the acid. None of them did, so I concluded that they were all sandstone. Although this was not limestone, I still found the sandstone outcrops worth visiting.

References: Penick, 1992; USGS, 2005

42. Lexington Fossils and Calcite

This is a long outcrop, and eastern sections are away from the highway.

County: Rockbridge County
Site type: Roadcut
Land status: Highway right-of-way, land not posted
Material: Fossils and calcite
Host rock: Ordovician Martinsburg and Oranda Formations black shale and limestone
Difficulty: Medium
Family-friendly: Yes
Tools needed: Hammer
Special concerns: Rocks are relatively barren
Special attractions: Natural Bridge
GPS parking: N37°45'39" / W79°25'22"
Topographic quadrangle: Lexington, VA

Finding the site: From I-81, take exit 188B to US-60 W. Continue 0.7 mile, and park on the right (north) side of US-60 W. The roadcut is just west of the parking area.

Rockhounding

This is Site 6 in Burns (1991). This is an easy roadcut to reach and is just off I-81. It is a good stop when you are traveling through western Virginia. The rocks are relatively barren of fossils, but this is common in shales. The beds dip steeply, so keep in mind that you are walking either up or down the section as you walk along the highway. Sometimes barren rock will quickly transition to a fossiliferous zone, and many times the fossil zones are thin and easily missed. The most abundant fossils are in the darker shales, and you often have to split the rocks to find the fossils. Most of the fossils are small brachiopods. The calcite is fairly abundant and easy to spot against the background of the dark shale and limestone.

The outcrop is a long exposure. Burns (1991) stated that the rocks in the western roadcut had more fossils and included bryozoans, but I did not find

Many of the fossils are small and take some effort to find.

White calcite is common at this site and is a nice addition to the fossils.

any fossils other than brachiopods at this locality. Additional fossils zones may be found as you head further west along the roadcut, but the cut becomes much closer to the highway, and I recommend staying away from these sections to be safe.

References: Burns, 1991; USGS, 2005

Sites 42–43

43. Effinger Fossils

The fossils are generally found as loose rocks in reddish-brown soil.

See map page 186.
County/City: Rockbridge County
Site type: Roadcut
Land status: Private, appears to be in road right-of-way
Material: Fossils
Host rock: Ordovician Edinburg Formation, Lincolnshire and New Market Limestones
Difficulty: Hard
Family-friendly: No
Tools needed: Hammer
Special concerns: Site is close to road, fossil is hard to find
Special attractions: Natural Bridge
GPS parking: N37°45′39″ / W79°32′58″
GPS outcrops: N37°45′37″ / W79°32′54″

The fossils are found along the roadcut just east of the "Watch for Fallen Rocks" sign.

Topographic quadrangle: Collierstown, VA
Finding the site: From Lexington, start at the intersection of US-11 and VA-251. Take VA-251 west for 7.3 miles. We parked at the southern end of the parking lot for the Effinger Volunteer Fire Department as it appeared to have lots of space and we could park well away from their building. Walk across VA-251. The fossils are in the outcrops southeast of the parking area.

Rockhounding

This is Site 1 in Burns 1991. It was very difficult to find the fossils at this site and I was not able to find any fossils in the outcrop. The fossils at this locality are found as loose rocks in the reddish sandy soil along the roadcut. The pieces are generally fist-sized or smaller and contain brachiopods. The best way to spot the fossils is to look for gray to light orange pieces against the dark gray limestone. The area is also brushy and close to the road, so you should wear a safety vest, long pants, and gloves.

The best fossils are found by scouring the ground turning over rocks and brush. It took a while before I found fossils at this site. Once you understand

Look for areas of reddish-brown soil to find the fossils. This area is close to the road and you must be extremely careful of traffic.

how they occur and look for the gray to light orange pieces in the reddish soil, you should be able to find many pieces. It would be good to find some larger pieces and break them apart, as these may reveal larger fossils inside of the rocks. Some of the rocks are aggregates of fossils and breaking them apart may reveal interiors of brachiopods and other fossils.

References: Burns, 1991; USGS, 2005

44. Callie Furnace Slag and Limonite

The furnace is still standing and the area is overgrown with trees and brush.

County: Botetourt County
Site type: Former iron furnace and slag dump
Land status: Jefferson National Forest
Material: Slag and limonite
Host rock: Silurian and Devonian Sediments, Helderberg and Cayugan Groups
Difficulty: Easy
Family-friendly: Yes, but requires some hiking
Tools needed: Hammer
Special concerns: Fairly long hike to furnace, remote area
Special attractions: None
GPS parking: N37°46'51" / W79°49'25"
GPS furnace: N37°46'38" / W79°49'25"

Some of the glassy slag has iridescence revealed when broken and observed in bright sunlight.

Topographic quadrangle: Clifton Forge, VA
Finding the site: You can approach this area from Iron Gate or Glen Wilton. We chose to come in from Iron Gate since we were coming from the north. From I-64, take exit 27 for VA-629 toward US-60 Business W/US 220S. Go 0.6 mile, and turn right onto the US 220 Ramp to Iron Gate/Roanoke. Get on US 220 S and continue for 1.2 miles. Take the right fork (south) onto Earnest Avenue, and continue for 0.4 mile. Turn right (north) onto Wintergreen Avenue and continue for 0.5 mile to the intersection with Callie Mines Road, which is VA-835. Wintergreen Avenue loops back southwestward. Stay to the left to continue on Callie Mines Road southwest for about 1 mile.

You will come to a sign that says end of state maintenance. This is at N37°47'31" / W79°48'50." You can elect to stop here and hike, but my wife insisted on driving further. The road is not great, but we did fine with a Honda CR-V, and this has reasonable clearance. We continued about 1 mile and I finally decided it was safest to park and then walk. We parked just west of a powerline that crossed the road. From here, you can continue

Limonite and hematite can often be found along the road to Callie Furnace.

to hike on the level road to the furnace. It is approximately 1 more mile. The road is likely passable by most vehicles, but it ends at a gate and vehicles can pass no further. From the gate, continue on the road for about 500 feet, and the furnace is to your left (south). The large slag pile is just south of the furnace.

This was a fair amount of hiking. It may be better to approach this from the opposite direction, but this road also appeared rough, based on what we saw from the furnace. Either way you will need to hike to the furnace. This can be a tricky place to find so I highly recommend planning your route in advance through Google Maps or a similar method.

Rockhounding

This is a former furnace in a remote area of Virginia. It remains largely intact but overgrown by vegetation. Unlike the numerous furnaces that served the Confederacy, this furnace was built after the Civil War. Callie Furnace was built as a hot-blast charcoal furnace around 1873–1874, and it was built for D.S. Cook of Wrightsville, Pennsylvania. It is notable that this was a Virginia

The slag dump is extensive and can be seen through the woods from the furnace and on satellite photographs.

furnace built for a Pennsylvanian operator during the Reconstruction Period, which lasted from 1865 to 1877.

By 1876 Callie Furnace was enlarged and converted into a coke furnace. The furnace produced mill pig iron, which was transported to mills in Ohio and Pennsylvania. The furnace went out of blast in 1884. Callie Furnace had a short operating life and it could not compete with the new iron facilities that were starting elsewhere in the United States.

This was the largest furnace in the area, and it processed limonite and other iron ores from nearby iron mines. Most of the ore is from Silurian–Devonian sediments. We did not find any mines in the furnace area, but the ground surrounding the furnace had pieces of limonite, and we found some colorful, dense limonite and hematite pieces on the hike to the furnace.

The furnace area has picnic tables and an iron platform. The iron platform appears to be of relatively recent construction (less than 50 years old). The slag pile is extensive and is southeast of the furnace. It is almost entirely barren of vegetation, despite being in the forest for nearly 150 years. Mine waste dumps are often overgrown with vegetation, but this slag does not allow plants to grow. Fortunately it was mainly from the processing of iron, not sulfide minerals, and most of the slag is glassy or otherwise intact so as not to leach and poison the surrounding area. An iron ore processing facility could never dispose of slag in that manner today in the United States.

You can easily find interesting pieces of slag in the slag dump. Many of them are glassy and green. There is quite a bit of dark gray dull slag as well, but with some effort you can find the glassy pieces with flow banding. Many of the pieces have a conchoidal fracture similar to the bottom of a broken coke bottle. The slag dump is easy to spot on a satellite photograph on Google Maps and is useful as a guide to finding the furnace.

References: Lesure, 1957; NPS, 1974; USGS, 2005

Sites 44–47

45. Roaring Run Furnace Glassy Slag

Glassy black and green slag can be seen on the trail next to the furnace.

See map page 195.
County: Botetourt County
Site type: Former iron furnace and slag dump
Land status: George Washington National Forest
Material: Slag and limonite
Host rock: Silurian and Devonian Sediments, Helderberg and Cayugan Groups
Difficulty: Easy
Family-friendly: Yes
Tools needed: None, no collecting allowed
Special concerns: None
Special attractions: Roaring Run Falls
GPS parking: N37°42'23" / W79°53'36"

The remains of the furnace are well preserved and maintained by the Forest Service.

GPS Furnace: N37°42'26" / W79°53'35"
Topographic quadrangle: Strom, VA
Finding the site: From Eagle Rock, take US-220 to the intersection with VA-615. Take 615 northwest for 5.5 miles. Turn right (north) onto VA-621. Proceed 0.9 mile on VA-621, which is Roaring Run Road, and turn left (west) at the sign for Roaring Run Furnace. Continue 0.2 mile to the parking area. From here you can follow the signs to the furnace and other trails in the area.

Rockhounding

Roaring Run Furnace is located in a Day Use Area in Jefferson National Forest. As such, it has excellent parking, a restroom, and well-marked trails to Roaring Run Furnace and Roaring Run Falls. The furnace is a short hike from the parking area.

Roaring Run was a hot-blast charcoal furnace that was built around 1832. The furnace processed "brown hematite ore" from an ore bank one mile south of the furnace. It was abandoned in 1854, and information from Lesley (1859) indicates that the furnace was dilapidated by 1859.

Glassy black and green slag is easy to see on the ground near the furnace.

This is an old furnace and predates the Civil War. The furnace still stands and while surrounded by a wood fence you can still walk up to it. The furnace is surrounded by hundreds of tons of glassy slag. Most of the slag is black, but green pieces with flow banding are abundant. Most of the pieces are 1 to 3 inches wide. They are easily seen on the trails around the furnace.

Many of the older furnaces that I have visited tend to have glassy and colorful slag. The furnaces of the late nineteenth and early twentieth centuries tend to have ugly gray rough slag, while the furnaces of the late eighteenth and early nineteenth centuries have glassy colorful slag. I have seen this in other states as well. The furnaces from the late 1700s to the early 1800s in New York state often produced bright blue slag.

We did not see any limonite on the trails, but I noticed that a creek next to the furnace was bright orange. This creek had very steep banks and it was not possible to climb down for a closer look. The orange water is usually seen in areas with acid mine drainage. The rocks in the area are not high in sulfides, so it probably is not sulfuric acid drainage, but may be related to leaching of limonitic rocks.

We did not get to walk to Roaring Run Falls, but I am sure this would have been a good side trip if we had the opportunity. We also noticed that they had a trail called the Iron Ore Trail. This trail appeared to lead to Iron Ore Knob. No mines are marked on the topographic map in this area, but any place with the name Iron Ore Knob would be a good place to check out. We walked up the trail and soon found it blocked by a fallen tree. At that point we quit and left this for another day.

As we were walking to the furnace we met a family that was walking back to the parking lot. A boy of about 6 years old had found a rock near the furnace and wanted to know what it was. His father did not know. My wife pointed at me and said, "Ask him, he is a geologist." I told the boy and his father that it was a piece of glassy slag and that it came from the processing of the iron in the furnace. I told him it was an excellent piece. The little boy was very excited and very proud that he had found something good. It felt good to offer encouragement to a young person and contribute in a small way to what I hope was a memorable family trip. I did not tell him that collecting was not allowed at the site as this would have spoiled the trip for everyone. I am sure that many kids who visit this site pick up the glassy slag, and with hundreds of tons of glass around the furnace, it is going to be there for a long time.

References: Beard, 2014; Lesure, 1957; USGS, 2001; USGS, 2005

46. Rich Patch Banded Sediments

The banding is due to varying amounts of limonite and hematite staining in the sediments.

See map page 195.
County: Botetourt County
Site type: Roadcut
Land status: George Washington National Forest
Material: Banded sediments
Host rock: Silurian Sediments of the Keefer, Rose Hill, and Tuscarora Formations
Difficulty: Easy
Family-friendly: No. Too close to traffic and potential rockfalls from cliff
Tools needed: Hammer and chisel
Special concerns: Traffic along VA-621
Special attractions: Roaring Run Furnace and Falls
GPS parking: N37°42'44" / W79°54'35"
Topographic quadrangle: Strom, VA

The shaley zones tend to be the most colorful and are also subject to most of the erosion.

Finding the site: From Eagle Rock, take US-220 to the intersection at VA-615. Take 615 northwest for 5.5 miles. Turn right (north) onto VA-621. Proceed 2.8 miles on VA-621, which is Roaring Run Road. The long roadcut of banded sediments is on the east side of the road. Parking is at the northern end of the roadcut.

Rockhounding

This is a long roadcut that has decorative rocks. The roadcut is through a colorful series of Silurian shales, siltstones, and sandstones that are shades of white, orange, red, green, and brown. The sediments are almost entirely clastic, and I did not see any limestones in the cut. I also did not see any fossils.

The sediments dip approximately 45 degrees to the south and strike perpendicular to the road. This maximizes the layers of sediment that you can see in the section. The most colorful sediments are the softer, less–resistant shales between the harder, more resistant sandstones. Not all of the rocks are banded,

This sandstone shows zones of white, yellow, and red and is typical of the color bands at this site.

and you have to look for the best pieces to break off the outcrops. While the softer shales erode quicker than the sandstones, many of the shales are still durable and make good display pieces.

Reference: USGS, 2005

47. Covington Ochre and Limonite

Much of the outcrop is soft material that could make a good orange to red pigment.

See map page 195.
County: Alleghany County
Site type: Roadcut
Land status: George Washington National Forest
Material: Ochre and limonite
Host rock: Silurian Sediments of the Keefer, Rose Hill, and Tuscarora Formations
Difficulty: Easy
Family-friendly: Yes
Tools needed: Hammer and chisel
Special concerns: Ticks and briars
Special attractions: Dolly Ann Roadless Area
GPS parking: N37°48′25″ / W79°55′34″
Topographic quadrangle: Covington, VA
Finding the site: From I-64, take exit 16 A as you approach Covington. Follow US-60 west for 0.6 mile and turn right (north) on East Dolly Ann Drive. Go about

The outcrops are covered by vegetation and you have to climb through briars to get to the rocks.

300 feet, and turn right to stay on Dolly Ann Drive. This is the same as VA-625. Continue for 3.7 miles. The road is relatively featureless as it is straight and in the valley of Ponding Mill Creek. Park at the GPS coordinates on the left (north) side of the road, and look for a small overhang with a pile of rocks that resembles a small prospect pit. It may or may not have dripping water. From here, walk about 100 feet southwest along Dolly Mill Drive, and look for outcrops of reddish-orange rocks. This is the ochre and limonite.

Rockhounding

Ochre is an earthen pigment formed from ferric oxides and hydroxides. It is the oldest known pigment and has been used for coloring from the beginning of history through the present. Ochre comes in various shades of yellow, orange, red, and brown.

At this site, the ochre can be dug out of the base of the cliff, and it is also adjacent to hard and intact outcrops of limonite. Some of the limonite can also be crushed to make a yellow ochre. Much of the softer material at this roadcut is reddish brown.

The ochre is soft and the outcrop is easily broken apart with a hammer.

Ochre is common in this part of Virginia. The town of Paint Bank, located about 30 miles southwest, was named for the deposits of ochre along the banks of Potts Creek. The area northeast of Covington has several other iron mines. These are mainly mines that worked the deposits of iron oxides in Silurian/Devonian sediments and these likely have significant amounts of ochre as well.

References: Lesure, 1981; USGS, 2005

48. Peters Mountain Limonite

The limonite is found both on the road and alongside the road near a sharp turn to the north.

County: Alleghany County
Site type: Roadcut
Land status: George Washington National Forest
Material: Limonite
Host rock: Silurian and Devonian sediments
Difficulty: Easy
Family-friendly: Yes
Tools needed: Hammer with a pointed end
Special concerns: Rocks are also found in the road, must not block any vehicles
Special attractions: None
GPS parking: N37°37'40" / W80°11'10"
Topographic quadrangle: Alleghany, VA-WV
Finding the site: From I-64, take exit 16 A as you approach Covington. Follow US-60 west for 0.9 mile and turn left (south) on Madison Street, which is the same as VA-18S. Go about 300 feet, and turn right to stay on Dolly Ann Drive. This is the

same as VA-625. Continue for 19.7 miles on VA-18. Turn right (west) onto FR 350. This is an indistinct gravel road and is easy to miss. Continue north on this road for about 0.3 mile. The limonite is found in the road bed and along the road side as the road makes a turn to the north. The road becomes darker orange in this area, indicating the presence of iron minerals.

Rockhounding

Peters Mountain is known for limonite and hematite, but it is a very long mountain and sections can be difficult to access. This Forest Service Road is relatively good but it is several miles long and I did not get to investigate all of the sections. Some of the limonite and hematite are iridescent, and I had hoped to find some former mines to explore.

I was not able to get to any of the mines but found that limonite is common along this road. Like many mining districts, the access roads cut through mineralized areas, and representative ore minerals can sometimes be found both within and adjacent to the roads.

At this locality pieces of limonite are found as some of the road aggregate and along the side of the road. It is easy to find large hand samples

Some of the limonite on Peters Mountain exhibits iridescence.

Many of the best pieces are found in the road bed, especially where the road has a slight orange tint from iron mineralization.

protruding from the roadbed, and many of these are dense and contain significant amounts of limonite and goethite. You can pick up the loose pieces but in most cases you need a small tool to dislodge the buried rocks.

One of the pieces of the former iron ores that I found in the roadbed had iridescence. This indicated to me that I was in the right area to find more iridescent pieces, although I did not find any. It would take some more effort but it would be great to find an actual former mine site that can be accessed. I tried to go to some of the mines marked on the topographic map but found that many of them were on private land, despite being mapped as George Washington National Forest in Google Maps. If you do collect any rocks from the roadbed, be sure to cover any holes to make sure that you do not start a pothole. Rain will wash out and expand any holes in the road, so it is important to leave the road as you found it.

References: Lesure, 1981; Penick, 1987; USGS, 2005

Site 48

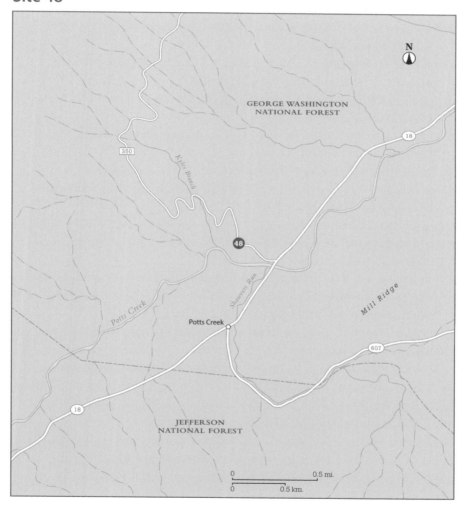

REFERENCES

Beard, Robert D. 2014. *Rockhounding New York.* Guilford, CT: Falcon Guides.

Beard, Robert D. 2015. *Rockhounding Delaware, Maryland, and the Washington DC Area.* Guilford, CT: Falcon Guides.

Bernstein, Lawrence R. 1980. *Minerals of the Washington, DC Area.* Maryland Geological Survey Educational Series No. 5.

Brown, A., H. L. Berryhill Jr., D. A. Taylor, and J. V. A. Trumbull. 1952. *Coal Resources of Virginia.* U.S. Geological Survey Circular 171, 57 p.

Burns, Jasper. 1991. *Fossil Collecting in the Mid-Atlantic States.* Baltimore, MD: John Hopkins University Press.

Eckert, Allan W. 2000. *Earth Treasures Volume 2, the Southeastern Quadrant.* Lincoln, NE: iUniverse.com.

Frye, Keith. 1986. *Roadside Geology of Virginia.* Missoula, MT: Mountain Press.

Henika, W. S. 1971. *Geology of the Basset quadrangle, Virginia, Report of investigations.* Virginia Division of Mineral Resources 26.

Hobbs, Carl. 2009. "York River Geology." *Journal of Coastal Research,* no. 57: 10–16.

Huber, King N., and W. W. Eckhardt. 1999. "Devils Postpile Story, Sequoia Natural History Association." *Sequoia Natural History Association.*

Knechtel, Maxwell M. 1943. "Manganese deposits of the Lyndhurst–Vesuvius district, Augusta and Rockbridge Counties, Virginia, Strategic Minerals Investigations." *USGS Bulletin* 940-F, 163–98.

Kuff, Karen R., and James R. Brooks. 2007. *Building Stones of Maryland.* Maryland Geological Survey Pamphlet Series.

Lesley, Peter J. 1859. *The Iron Manufacturer's Guide to the Furnaces, Forges and Rolling Mills of the United States.* New York: John Wiley.

Lesure, F. G. 1957. *Geology of the Clifton Forge iron district, Virginia: Virginia Polytechnic Institute Bulletin.* Engineering Experiment Station Series no. ll8, 130 p.

Lesure, F. G. 1981. *Geologic map of the Dolly Ann Roadless Area, Alleghany County, Virginia.* U.S. Geological Survey Miscellaneous Field Studies Map MF-1358-A, scale 1:24,000.

Mitchell, R. S. 1967. "Tridymite pseudomorphs after wood in Virginian Lower Cretaceous sediments." *Science,* Nov 17: 905–6.

Mixon, R. B., D. L. Southwick, and J. C. Read. 1972. Geologic map of the Quantico quadrangle, Prince William and Stafford Counties, Virginia, and Charles County, Maryland, U.S. Geological Survey Quadrangle Map GQ-1044, scale 1:24,000.

Moore, C. H. Jr. 1937. "The staurolite area of Patrick and Henry Counties, Virginia." *American Mineralogist* 22, 990.

National Park Service, Draft Nomination for Elizabeth Furnace, 085-940, available at http://www.dhr.virginia.gov/registers/Counties/Shenandoah/085-0940_Elizabeth_Furnace_1999_Draft_Nomination.pdf, 1999.

National Park Service, Final Nomination for Callie Furnace, 011-0065, available at http://www.dhr.virginia.gov/registers/Counties/Botetourt/011-0065_Callie_Furnace_1974_Final_Nomination.pdf, 1974.

National Park Service, Final Nomination for Confederate Gun Mounts and Freestone Point, 076-0264, available at http://www.dhr.virginia.gov/registers/Counties/PrinceWilliam/076-0264_Confederate_Gun_Mounts_at_Freestone_Point_1989_Final_Nomination.pdf, 1989.

Penick, D. Allen Jr. February 1987. "Virginia Mineral Locality Index." *Virginia Minerals*. 33, no. 1.

Penick, D. Allen Jr. August, 1992. "Gemstones and Decorative-Ornamental Stones of Virginia." *Virginia Minerals* 38, no. 3.

Rader, E. K., and T. H. Biggs. 1975. *Geology of the Front Royal, Virginia 7.5-minute quadrangle.* Virginia Division of Mineral Resources, Report of Investigations No. 40.

Rader, E. K., and T. H. Biggs. 1976. *Geology of the Strasburg and Toms Brook, Virginia 7.5-minute quadrangles.* Virginia Division of Mineral Resources, Report of Investigations No. 45.

Rader, E. K., and W. J. Perry Jr. 1976. "Reinterpretation of the geology of Brocks Gap, Rockingham County, Virginia." *Virginia Minerals* 22, 37–45.

Reed, J. C., Jr., and Janice Jolly. 1963. Crystalline rocks of the Potomac River Gorge near Washington, DC. US Geological Survey Professional Paper 414-H, 16 p.

Roberts, J. K. 1934. "Virginia staurolites as gems." *American Mineralogist* 19, 549.

Robertson, R. 1885. *An examination of blue quartz from Nelson County,* Virginia: The Virginias, Vol. 6, p. 2–3.

Say, T. 1824. "An account of some of the fossil shells of Maryland." *Journal of the Academy of Natural Sciences of Philadelphia*, 1st series, 4: 124–55.

Southworth, S., W. C. Burton, J. S. Schindler, and A. J. Froelich. 1999. *Digital Geologic Map of Loudoun County, Virginia.* US Geological Survey Open-File Report 99-150.

Spears, D. B., B. E. Owens, and C. M. Bailey. 2004. The Goochland-Chopawamsic Terrane Boundary, Central Virginia Piedmont, in Geology of the National Capital Region— Field Trip Guidebook, Circular 1264, United States Geologic Survey.

United States Geological Survey. 1998. *Building Stones of Our Nation's Capital.* Reston, VA: US Geological Survey, p. 36.

United States Geological Survey. 2001. Silent Reminders, Geologic Wonders of the George Washington and Jefferson National Forests, No. 3 in a Series.

United States Geological Survey. 2005. Open-File Report 2005-1325. Preliminary integrated geologic map databases for the United States: Delaware, Maryland, New York, Pennsylvania, and Virginia.

Virginia Division of Mineral Resources. 2003. *Digital Representation of the 1993 Geologic Map of Virginia*. Virginia Division of Mineral Resources Publication 174, compact disc.

Ward, L. W., and B. W. Blackwelder, Chesapecten. 1975. A new genus of Pectinidae (Mollusca: Bivalvia) from the Miocene and Pliocene of eastern North America. U. S. Geological Survey Professional Paper 861, 24 p, 7 pl.

Werner, H. J. 1966. *Geology of the Vesuvius Quadrangle, Report of Investigations 7*. Virginia Department of Mineral Resources.

Wilkes, G. P., E. W. Spencer, Nick H. Evans, and E. V. M. Campbell. 2007. *Geology of Rockbridge County*. Virginia Department of Mines, Minerals, and Energy Publication 170.

Wise, Michael A. 1981. "Blue Quartz in Virginia." *Virginia Minerals* 27, no. 2, 9–12.

Withington, C. F. 1975. Building stones of our nation's capital. US Geological Survey, p. 44.

SITE INDEX

INDEX

ABOUT THE AUTHOR

Robert Beard is a geologist and has collected rocks for over thirty years. He received his BA in geology, with a minor in mathematics, from California State University, Chico, in 1983 and his MS in geology from the University of New Mexico in 1987. He is a licensed professional geologist in Pennsylvania and works in the environmental consulting industry. He has collected rocks throughout the United States, Caribbean, and parts of Europe. He is a contributor to *Rock & Gem* magazine and has written for *Rock & Gem* since 1993. His most recent books for FalconGuides include *Rockhounding Pennsylvania and New Jersey*, published in 2013, *Rockhounding New York*, published in 2014, and *Rockhounding Delaware, Maryland, and the Washington DC Metro Area*, published in 2015. He and his wife, Rosalina, lives in Harrisburg, Pennsylvania, with the chihuahuas, Nema and Little One, and Lennon the cat.

Credit: Rosalina Beard